Guide to Writing a Novel With ChatGPT

GUIDE TO WRITING A NOVEL WITH CHATGPT

First edition. March 25, 2024.

ISBN: 979-8224349104

Written by J. Sagel.

Chapter 1: Introduction - The Power of AI in Fiction Writing

Part 1: Unleashing Creativity: Harnessing ChatGPT for Inspired Storytelling

IN THE VAST LANDSCAPE of fiction writing, creativity serves as the cornerstone of captivating storytelling. From crafting compelling characters to weaving intricate plot lines, the ability to conjure imaginative worlds and narratives is paramount. However, for many writers, tapping into this wellspring of creativity can prove to be a daunting task, often plagued by bouts of writer's block or the struggle to find inspiration.

Enter ChatGPT, an AI-powered writing assistant developed by OpenAI. ChatGPT represents a groundbreaking advancement in the field of artificial intelligence, capable of generating human-like text based on the input it receives. With its vast repository of knowledge and language proficiency, ChatGPT serves as a valuable resource for writers seeking to enhance their creative endeavors.

At its core, ChatGPT operates on a simple premise: to assist writers in generating ideas, refining prose, and overcoming obstacles encountered during the writing process. By leveraging state-of-the-art machine learning algorithms, ChatGPT analyzes text input and generates contextually relevant responses, mimicking the conversational style of human communication. This unique ability makes ChatGPT an invaluable tool for writers seeking inspiration, feedback, or guidance in their creative pursuits.

The allure of ChatGPT lies in its versatility and adaptability to various writing styles and genres. Whether you're crafting a fantasy epic, a science fiction thriller, or a contemporary romance novel, ChatGPT can seamlessly integrate into your creative workflow, offering insights and suggestions tailored to your specific needs. Its ability to emulate different voices and perspectives adds depth and authenticity to the writing process, enabling writers to explore new narrative avenues and experiment with diverse storytelling techniques.

One of the most remarkable aspects of ChatGPT is its capacity to generate original ideas and concepts based on the prompts provided by the user. By engaging in dialogue with ChatGPT, writers can stimulate their creativity and brainstorm new plot points, character traits, or thematic elements for their stories. Whether you're struggling to develop a compelling protagonist or devising an intricate plot twist, ChatGPT can serve as a collaborative partner, sparking inspiration and fueling your creative imagination.

Furthermore, ChatGPT's ability to generate coherent and grammatically correct text in real-time facilitates a seamless writing experience for authors. Gone are the days of staring at a blank page, grappling with the daunting task of putting pen to paper. With ChatGPT by your side, you can embark on your writing journey with confidence, knowing that you have a reliable companion to assist you every step of the way.

It's important to note that while ChatGPT excels at generating text based on the input it receives, it is not a substitute for human creativity or intuition. Instead, it should be viewed as a complementary tool that enhances the creative process by providing inspiration, guidance, and feedback. Ultimately, the responsibility for shaping and refining the final narrative rests with the writer, who must exercise discernment and artistic judgment in incorporating ChatGPT's suggestions into their work.

In the following chapters, we will delve deeper into the myriad ways in which ChatGPT can be utilized to enhance your fiction writing endeavors. From character development to plot construction, dialogue crafting to world-building, we will explore practical strategies and techniques for harnessing the full potential of ChatGPT as a creative ally. By embracing the power of AI in fiction writing, you can unlock new realms of imagination and embark on a transformative journey of literary exploration and discovery.

Part 2: Understanding AI Writing Assistants: Demystifying ChatGPT

AS WRITERS EMBARK ON their creative journey with ChatGPT, it's essential to gain a deeper understanding of how AI writing assistants function and the underlying principles that govern their operation. By demystifying the inner workings of ChatGPT, writers can better leverage its capabilities and maximize its potential as a creative tool.

At its core, ChatGPT is powered by a sophisticated neural network architecture known as the Transformer model. Developed by researchers at Google, the Transformer model revolutionized the field of natural language processing by introducing a novel mechanism for processing sequential data. Unlike traditional recurrent neural networks (RNNs) or long short-term memory (LSTM) networks, which suffer from issues such as vanishing gradients and difficulty in capturing long-range dependencies, the Transformer model relies on self-attention mechanisms to process input sequences in parallel, enabling more efficient and effective language understanding.

Central to the functioning of ChatGPT is its ability to generate text based on the context provided by the user. This process begins with the user inputting a prompt or query, which serves as the starting point for generating a response. The prompt is then encoded into a numerical representation known as an embedding, which is fed into the Transformer model. The model processes the embedding through multiple layers of self-attention and feedforward neural networks, gradually transforming the input into a sequence of tokens representing the generated text.

During the generation process, ChatGPT utilizes a technique known as autoregressive decoding, whereby it predicts each token in the sequence based on the preceding tokens. This sequential generation strategy allows ChatGPT to generate coherent and contextually relevant responses that closely mimic human language patterns. By considering the context provided by the user input, ChatGPT is able to generate text that is syntactically and semantically consistent, enhancing the overall coherence and readability of the output.

One of the key advantages of ChatGPT is its ability to generate diverse and varied responses to the same prompt. This variability stems from the stochastic nature of the generation process, wherein the model samples from a probability distribution over the vocabulary at each step. By incorporating randomness into the generation process, ChatGPT is able to produce a wide range of potential responses, offering writers multiple options to choose from and fostering creative exploration and experimentation.

However, it's important to note that while ChatGPT excels at generating text based on the input it receives, it is not infallible and may occasionally produce nonsensical or inappropriate responses. This phenomenon, known as "hallucination" or "mode collapse," occurs when the model generates text that is unrelated to the input prompt or deviates from the intended context. To mitigate this issue, writers can employ techniques such as prompt engineering, where they carefully craft prompts to guide the model towards desired responses, or fine-tuning, where they train the model on specific datasets to improve its performance in a particular domain.

Another consideration when working with ChatGPT is the potential for biases and stereotypes to manifest in the generated text. Like all machine learning models, ChatGPT learns from the data it is trained on, which may contain inherent biases present in society. As a result, ChatGPT may inadvertently reproduce or amplify these biases in its output, leading to the propagation of harmful stereotypes or misinformation. To address this issue, researchers and developers must prioritize ethical considerations in the design and deployment of AI writing assistants, implementing safeguards and mitigation strategies to minimize the impact of biases on the generated text.

Despite these challenges, ChatGPT represents a powerful tool for writers seeking to enhance their creative process and overcome obstacles encountered during the writing journey. By understanding the underlying mechanisms of AI writing assistants like ChatGPT, writers can harness the full potential of these technologies to unlock new realms of imagination and innovation in their fiction writing endeavors. In the following chapters, we will delve deeper into practical strategies and techniques for effectively integrating ChatGPT into your creative workflow, empowering you to unleash your full creative potential and craft compelling narratives that captivate and inspire readers.

Part 3: Embracing Innovation: How AI is Revolutionizing the Writing Process

IN THE EVER-EVOLVING landscape of fiction writing, the emergence of AI-powered writing assistants like ChatGPT represents a paradigm shift in the way stories are conceived, crafted, and shared with the world. By embracing the transformative potential of AI, writers can revolutionize their writing process, unlock new avenues of creativity, and push the boundaries of storytelling to unprecedented heights.

One of the most significant ways in which AI is revolutionizing the writing process is by democratizing access to tools and resources that were once exclusive to professional writers or established authors. With AI writing assistants like ChatGPT, aspiring writers and seasoned veterans alike can access a wealth of knowledge, guidance, and inspiration at their fingertips, leveling the playing field and empowering individuals from diverse backgrounds to pursue their creative aspirations.

Moreover, AI writing assistants offer writers unparalleled flexibility and adaptability, allowing them to tailor their writing experience to their specific needs and preferences. Whether you prefer to brainstorm ideas collaboratively with ChatGPT, receive real-time feedback on your writing, or explore new narrative directions and plot twists, AI writing assistants can accommodate a wide range of creative workflows, providing support and guidance every step of the way.

Furthermore, AI writing assistants enable writers to break free from traditional constraints and explore unconventional storytelling formats and narrative structures. From interactive storytelling experiences to multimedia-rich narratives incorporating text, images, and audio, the possibilities for experimentation and innovation are virtually limitless. By embracing AI as a creative partner, writers can push the boundaries of storytelling and engage readers in new and exciting ways, fostering a deeper sense of immersion and interactivity.

Another key benefit of AI-powered writing assistants is their ability to enhance collaboration and foster community among writers. Through online platforms and forums dedicated to AI writing, writers can connect with peers, share ideas and feedback, and collaborate on collaborative writing projects. By leveraging the collective wisdom and creativity of a global community of writers, AI writing assistants can serve as catalysts for collaboration and collective creativity, driving innovation and pushing the boundaries of what's possible in fiction writing.

However, as with any technological innovation, the widespread adoption of AI writing assistants raises important ethical and societal considerations that must be carefully considered. Chief among these concerns is the potential impact of AI on the job market and the future of work, particularly in creative industries such as writing and publishing. While AI writing assistants can augment and enhance the creative process, they also raise concerns about job displacement and the devaluation of human creativity and craftsmanship.

Furthermore, the proliferation of AI-generated content raises thorny questions about authorship, ownership, and intellectual property rights. As AI writing assistants become increasingly adept at generating text that closely mimics human language, distinguishing between human-authored and AI-generated content may become more challenging, leading to potential disputes over attribution and copyright infringement. To address these concerns, policymakers, industry stakeholders, and content creators must work together to establish clear guidelines and standards for the ethical use of AI in writing and publishing.

Despite these challenges, the potential benefits of AI in revolutionizing the writing process far outweigh the risks. By embracing AI as a creative ally, writers can unlock new realms of imagination, push the boundaries of storytelling, and connect with audiences in profound and meaningful ways. Whether you're a seasoned author seeking to enhance your writing process or an aspiring writer looking to embark on your creative journey, AI writing assistants like ChatGPT offer a wealth of opportunities to explore, experiment, and innovate in the pursuit of literary excellence.

Chapter 2: Understanding Character Development with ChatGPT

Part 1: Creating Complex Characters: Using ChatGPT as a Character Building Tool

CHARACTER DEVELOPMENT lies at the heart of compelling fiction, as readers are drawn to well-rounded, multi-dimensional characters who undergo growth and transformation throughout the narrative. In this chapter, we will explore how ChatGPT can serve as a valuable tool for crafting complex and nuanced characters that resonate with readers on a deep emotional level.

When embarking on the journey of character development, writers often face the challenge of fleshing out their characters and imbuing them with depth, complexity, and authenticity. From protagonists grappling with inner conflicts and personal demons to antagonists driven by motives both dark and compelling, creating believable characters requires a keen understanding of human psychology, behavior, and motivation.

One of the key advantages of using ChatGPT for character development is its ability to simulate human-like interactions and responses, providing writers with valuable insights into the minds and personalities of their characters. By engaging in dialogue with ChatGPT, writers can explore various aspects of their characters' identities, including their desires, fears, aspirations, and vulnerabilities, helping to flesh out their motivations and internal struggles.

Moreover, ChatGPT can serve as a sounding board for writers to test out different character traits, quirks, and idiosyncrasies, allowing them to experiment with various personality types and behavioral patterns. Whether you're crafting a stoic hero with a tragic past, a charming rogue with a penchant for mischief, or a mysterious antagonist shrouded in enigma, ChatGPT can provide valuable feedback and suggestions to help you refine and develop your characters with depth and authenticity.

In addition to providing insights into individual characters, ChatGPT can also assist writers in creating dynamic relationships and interactions between characters. By simulating dialogue exchanges between characters, writers can explore the dynamics of interpersonal relationships, uncovering conflicts, tensions, and alliances that drive the narrative forward. Whether it's the banter between friends, the simmering tension between rivals, or the tender moments of intimacy between lovers, ChatGPT can help writers craft authentic and emotionally resonant interactions that enrich the storytelling experience.

Furthermore, ChatGPT can serve as a source of inspiration for character development, generating prompts and scenarios that challenge writers to delve deeper into their characters' psyches and explore untapped aspects of their personalities. Whether it's a hypothetical situation that tests a character's moral compass or a flashback that reveals a pivotal moment from their past, ChatGPT can spark creative ideas and provide writers with new avenues for character exploration and development.

However, it's important to approach character development with a critical eye and exercise discernment when incorporating ChatGPT's suggestions into your writing. While ChatGPT can offer valuable insights and inspiration, it is ultimately up to the writer to ensure that the characters remain consistent with the overarching narrative and serve the story's thematic and dramatic goals. By striking a balance between creative experimentation and narrative coherence, writers can harness the full potential of ChatGPT as a character building tool and create memorable and engaging characters that resonate with readers long after they've turned the final page.

Part 2: Exploring Motivations and Backstories: Deepening Characterization with AI

CHARACTER DEVELOPMENT is a multifaceted process that involves delving into the motivations, desires, and backstories of the characters inhabiting the fictional world. In this section, we will explore how ChatGPT can be utilized to deepen characterization by uncovering the intricate layers of a character's psyche and history.

At the core of every compelling character lies a set of motivations and desires that drive their actions and shape their journey throughout the narrative. By understanding what motivates a character, writers can imbue them with agency and purpose, creating characters who feel authentic and relatable to readers. ChatGPT can serve as a valuable tool for exploring these motivations, providing writers with prompts and questions that challenge them to delve deeper into their characters' innermost thoughts and desires.

For example, writers can use ChatGPT to generate prompts that probe into a character's goals, fears, and aspirations, prompting them to reflect on what drives their characters to pursue their objectives and overcome obstacles. By engaging in dialogue with ChatGPT, writers can uncover hidden layers of complexity within their characters, revealing underlying desires, insecurities, and conflicts that shape their decisions and behaviors.

Moreover, ChatGPT can assist writers in crafting compelling character backstories that provide context and depth to their personalities and motivations. By generating prompts that explore a character's past experiences, traumas, and formative moments, writers can flesh out their characters' histories and explore how past events have shaped their present selves. From childhood traumas to formative relationships, ChatGPT can help writers uncover the defining moments that have shaped their characters' identities and worldviews.

Additionally, ChatGPT can serve as a valuable resource for brainstorming and developing character arcs that chart the evolution and growth of characters over the course of the narrative. By generating prompts that challenge writers to envision the challenges and obstacles their characters must overcome, ChatGPT can help writers map out the trajectory of their characters' journeys, from their initial motivations and goals to the transformative experiences that propel them towards change and self-discovery.

One of the key benefits of using ChatGPT for character development is its ability to provide writers with fresh perspectives and insights into their characters' psyches. By engaging in dialogue with ChatGPT, writers can adopt different narrative voices and viewpoints, allowing them to explore their characters from multiple angles and uncover new facets of their personalities. Whether it's adopting the perspective of a supporting character or delving into the inner thoughts of an antagonist, ChatGPT can help writers gain a deeper understanding of their characters' motivations and perspectives, enriching the storytelling experience.

Furthermore, ChatGPT can serve as a valuable tool for generating character dialogue and monologue that captures the unique voice and personality of each character. By inputting snippets of dialogue or internal monologue, writers can receive feedback and suggestions from ChatGPT on how to refine and enhance their characters' speech patterns, mannerisms, and idiosyncrasies. Whether it's crafting witty banter between friends or capturing the introspective musings of a troubled protagonist, ChatGPT can help writers infuse their characters' dialogue with authenticity and depth.

However, it's important to approach character development with a critical eye and exercise discernment when incorporating ChatGPT's suggestions into your writing. While ChatGPT can offer valuable insights and inspiration, it is ultimately up to the writer to ensure that the characters remain consistent with the overarching narrative and serve the story's thematic and dramatic goals. By striking a balance between creative experimentation and narrative coherence, writers can harness the full potential of ChatGPT as a tool for deepening characterization and creating compelling and multi-dimensional characters that resonate with readers.

Part 3: Crafting Memorable Protagonists and Antagonists: A Step-by-Step Guide

IN THE REALM OF FICTION writing, protagonists and antagonists play pivotal roles in driving the narrative forward and engaging readers in the story. Crafting memorable protagonists and antagonists requires careful attention to detail, as well as an understanding of the motivations, conflicts, and dynamics that shape their interactions. In this section, we will explore a step-by-step guide for using ChatGPT to craft compelling protagonists and antagonists that captivate readers and propel the story towards its climax.

Step 1: Define Your Characters' Core Traits and Attributes

The first step in crafting memorable protagonists and antagonists is to define their core traits and attributes. Consider what sets your characters apart from one another and what drives their actions and decisions throughout the narrative. With ChatGPT's assistance, brainstorm a list of adjectives, personality traits, and defining characteristics that capture the essence of your characters. Whether it's a courageous hero with a tragic past or a cunning villain with a hidden agenda, articulate the key traits that distinguish your characters and shape their identities.

Step 2: Develop Your Characters' Motivations and Goals

Once you've established your characters' core traits, delve deeper into their motivations and goals. What drives your protagonists to embark on their journey, and what obstacles do they seek to overcome along the way? Conversely, what motivates your antagonists to oppose the protagonist, and what are their ultimate objectives? Use ChatGPT to generate prompts and questions that challenge you to explore your characters' innermost desires, fears, and aspirations, uncovering the driving forces behind their actions and decisions.

Step 3: Flesh Out Your Characters' Backstories and Histories

Next, flesh out your characters' backstories and histories to provide context and depth to their personalities and motivations. Use ChatGPT to generate prompts that explore your characters' past experiences, traumas, and formative moments, uncovering the defining events that have shaped their identities and worldviews. From childhood traumas to pivotal relationships, delve into the rich tapestry of your characters' histories, revealing the formative experiences that have shaped who they are today.

Step 4: Create Dynamic Relationships and Interactions

Characters don't exist in isolation; they exist within a web of relationships and interactions that shape their experiences and perceptions of the world. Use ChatGPT to simulate dialogue exchanges between your characters, exploring the dynamics of their interpersonal relationships and uncovering conflicts, tensions, and alliances that drive the narrative forward. Whether it's the bond between allies, the rivalry between adversaries, or the complexities of romantic entanglements, craft dynamic relationships and interactions that enrich the storytelling experience and deepen readers' engagement with the characters.

Step 5: Establish Character Arcs and Development

Finally, establish character arcs and development trajectories that chart the evolution and growth of your characters over the course of the narrative. Use ChatGPT to brainstorm potential character arcs, outlining the challenges, obstacles, and transformative experiences that propel your characters towards change and self-discovery. Whether it's a protagonist overcoming their inner demons and embracing their true potential or an antagonist grappling with the consequences of their actions and seeking redemption, craft character arcs that resonate with readers and evoke empathy and understanding.

Throughout the character development process, it's important to remain open to new ideas and insights that emerge through dialogue with ChatGPT. While you may have a clear vision for your characters, ChatGPT can offer valuable perspectives and suggestions that challenge your assumptions and push you to explore new narrative avenues. By embracing ChatGPT as a creative partner, you can unlock new realms of imagination and innovation in your character development process, creating protagonists and antagonists that resonate with readers long after they've turned the final page.

In conclusion, crafting memorable protagonists and antagonists requires a combination of creativity, empathy, and strategic planning. By leveraging ChatGPT as a tool for character development, writers can deepen their understanding of their characters' motivations, relationships, and growth trajectories, creating rich and multi-dimensional characters that captivate readers and drive the narrative forward. Whether you're crafting a heroic protagonist on a quest for redemption or a formidable antagonist driven by ambition and revenge, ChatGPT can serve as a valuable ally in your quest to create compelling and unforgettable characters that leave a lasting impression on readers.

Chapter 3: Crafting Dynamic Dialogue: Tips and Techniques

Part 1: Breathing Life into Conversations: Enhancing Dialogue with ChatGPT

DIALOGUE IS A FUNDAMENTAL element of fiction writing, serving as a primary means of character interaction, plot advancement, and world-building. Well-crafted dialogue can bring characters to life, convey emotions and subtext, and immerse readers in the fictional world. In this section, we will explore how writers can use ChatGPT to enhance their dialogue writing skills and create dynamic and engaging conversations that resonate with readers.

Understanding the Role of Dialogue

Before delving into the specifics of crafting dialogue with ChatGPT, it's important to understand the essential role that dialogue plays in storytelling. Dialogue serves several key functions in fiction writing:

1. Characterization: Dialogue offers insights into characters' personalities, motivations, and relationships through the way they speak and interact with others.

2. Plot Advancement: Dialogue can drive the plot forward by conveying crucial information, revealing conflicts, and introducing key plot points and developments.

3. World-Building: Dialogue provides opportunities to immerse readers in the fictional world by introducing cultural nuances, slang, and dialects unique to the setting.

4. Subtext and Theme: Dialogue can convey subtext and thematic elements through the use of metaphor, irony, and ambiguity, enriching the narrative with layers of meaning.

With these functions in mind, writers can use ChatGPT to enhance their dialogue writing skills and create conversations that are authentic, compelling, and emotionally resonant.

Generating Natural-Sounding Dialogue Prompts

One of the challenges writers face when crafting dialogue is ensuring that it sounds natural and authentic to the characters and setting. ChatGPT can assist writers in generating dialogue prompts that capture the tone, voice, and personality of their characters, helping to maintain consistency and coherence in the dialogue.

To generate natural-sounding dialogue prompts with ChatGPT, consider the following tips:

1. Input Character Profiles: Provide ChatGPT with detailed profiles of your characters, including their backgrounds, personalities, speech patterns, and mannerisms. This information will help ChatGPT generate dialogue prompts that are consistent with the characters' identities and motivations.

1. Set the Scene: Describe the setting, context, and emotional atmosphere of the scene to provide ChatGPT with the necessary context for generating dialogue. Whether it's a tense confrontation, a lighthearted banter, or an intimate conversation, setting the scene helps ChatGPT generate dialogue prompts that resonate with the tone and mood of the scene.

1. Use Visual Aids: Incorporate visual aids such as character sketches, setting descriptions, and mood boards to provide ChatGPT with additional context and inspiration for

generating dialogue prompts. Visual cues can help ChatGPT visualize the scene and characters, resulting in more vivid and immersive dialogue prompts.

1. Experiment with Dialogue Tags: Experiment with different dialogue tags, such as "said," "asked," "replied," "whispered," and "shouted," to vary the rhythm and pacing of the dialogue. ChatGPT can generate dialogue prompts with different dialogue tags to convey the characters' emotions and intentions more effectively.

By incorporating these techniques, writers can use ChatGPT to generate natural-sounding dialogue prompts that capture the essence of their characters and settings, enriching the storytelling experience and engaging readers in meaningful conversations.

Exploring Character Dynamics and Relationships

Dialogue offers writers the opportunity to explore the dynamics and relationships between characters, revealing conflicts, tensions, and alliances that drive the narrative forward. ChatGPT can assist writers in crafting dynamic and authentic character interactions by simulating dialogue exchanges between characters, helping to develop their relationships and advance the plot organically.

To explore character dynamics and relationships with ChatGPT, consider the following strategies:

1. Role-Playing Exercises:

Engage in role-playing exercises with ChatGPT to simulate dialogue exchanges between characters. Assign different personas and objectives to each character, and allow ChatGPT to generate dialogue prompts based on their interactions. Role-playing exercises can help writers explore the nuances of character dynamics and relationships, uncovering conflicts, tensions, and emotional undercurrents that shape the narrative.

2. Explore Conflict and Tension:

Use ChatGPT to generate dialogue prompts that explore conflicts, tensions, and power dynamics between characters. Whether it's a heated argument, a subtle power struggle, or a moment of reconciliation, dialogue prompts generated by ChatGPT can help writers navigate complex interpersonal relationships and create compelling character interactions that drive the plot forward.

3. Develop Subplots and Side Characters:

Use ChatGPT to brainstorm dialogue prompts for subplots and side characters, enriching the narrative with secondary storylines and diverse perspectives. By exploring the perspectives and motivations of supporting characters through dialogue, writers can deepen the complexity of the fictional world and enhance readers' understanding of the main characters' journey.

4. Foreshadowing and Symbolism:

Use ChatGPT to generate dialogue prompts that incorporate foreshadowing and symbolism, hinting at future plot developments and thematic elements. By weaving subtle hints and clues into character interactions, writers can create a sense of anticipation and intrigue that keeps readers engaged and invested in the story.

By leveraging ChatGPT to explore character dynamics and relationships, writers can create dynamic and multi-dimensional characters that resonate with readers and drive the narrative forward with compelling dialogue and authentic interactions. Through role-playing exercises, conflict exploration, and subplot development, writers can use ChatGPT to unlock new insights and possibilities for character-driven storytelling, enriching the narrative with depth, complexity, and emotional resonance.

Crafting Authentic Character Voices and Speech Patterns

One of the hallmarks of effective dialogue is creating authentic character voices and speech patterns that reflect the characters' personalities, backgrounds, and motivations. ChatGPT can assist writers in crafting authentic dialogue by generating prompts that capture the unique voice and tone of each character, helping to differentiate their speech patterns and mannerisms.

To craft authentic character voices and speech patterns with ChatGPT, consider the following techniques:

1. Character Profiles and Backgrounds: Provide ChatGPT with detailed profiles of your characters, including their backgrounds, personalities, and speech patterns. Use ChatGPT to generate dialogue prompts that reflect each character's unique voice, dialect, and mannerisms, ensuring consistency and authenticity in their speech throughout the narrative.

1. Experiment with Speech Patterns: Experiment with different speech patterns, vocabulary choices, and sentence structures to reflect the characters' personalities and backgrounds. Whether it's a formal aristocrat, a streetwise hustler, or a quirky eccentric, ChatGPT can generate dialogue prompts with diverse speech patterns and styles that capture the essence of each character.

3. Incorporate Cultural Nuances:
Incorporate cultural nuances, slang,
and dialects unique to the setting and
characters' backgrounds to enrich the
dialogue with authenticity and depth.
ChatGPT can generate dialogue
prompts that incorporate cultural
references and linguistic quirks,
enhancing the realism of the dialogue
and immersing readers in the fictional
world.
4. Use Character-Specific Idioms and

Expressions: Use ChatGPT to generate
dialogue prompts that incorporate
character-specific idioms, expressions,
and catchphrases that reflect their
personalities and worldviews. Whether
it's a stoic warrior with a penchant for
philosophical musings or a
wisecracking sidekick with a flair for
sarcasm, infuse the dialogue with
idiomatic expressions that add depth
and texture to the characters' speech.

By experimenting with speech patterns, cultural nuances, and character-specific idioms, writers can use ChatGPT to craft authentic character voices and speech patterns that resonate with readers.

Part 2: Crafting Engaging Dialogue: Strategies and Techniques

CRAFTING ENGAGING DIALOGUE is essential for captivating readers and bringing characters to life on the page. In this section, we will explore various strategies and techniques for using ChatGPT to elevate your dialogue writing skills and create dynamic and immersive conversations that resonate with readers.

1. Establish Character Voice and Personality

One of the keys to crafting engaging dialogue is ensuring that each character has a distinct voice and personality that shines through in their speech. ChatGPT can help writers develop character voice by generating dialogue prompts that reflect the unique traits, quirks, and mannerisms of each character.

To establish character voice with ChatGPT, consider the following strategies:

• Provide ChatGPT with detailed character profiles, including information about each character's background, personality, and speech patterns.

• Use ChatGPT to generate dialogue prompts that reflect each character's unique voice, incorporating specific vocabulary choices, sentence structures, and speech patterns.

• Experiment with different dialogue tags, such as "said," "asked," "replied," and "exclaimed," to convey the characters' emotions and intentions more effectively.

• Incorporate character-specific idioms, expressions, and catchphrases into the dialogue to add depth and authenticity to the characters' speech.

By leveraging ChatGPT to establish character voice, writers can create dialogue that feels authentic and true to each character's personality, enhancing the overall realism and immersion of the narrative.

1. Focus on Subtext and Nonverbal Cues

Effective dialogue goes beyond the words spoken and often relies on subtext and nonverbal cues to convey meaning and emotion. ChatGPT can assist writers in crafting dialogue that is rich in subtext and nuance by generating prompts that explore the underlying emotions and motivations driving the characters' interactions.

To focus on subtext and nonverbal cues with ChatGPT, consider the following techniques:

• Use ChatGPT to generate dialogue prompts that incorporate subtle hints and clues about the characters' thoughts, feelings, and intentions.

• Experiment with dialogue tags and descriptive language to convey the characters' body language, facial expressions, and gestures.

• Explore the use of pauses, hesitations, and silences in the dialogue to create tension and suspense.

• Use ChatGPT to generate prompts that explore the characters' internal monologue, revealing their innermost thoughts and emotions.

By incorporating subtext and nonverbal cues into the dialogue, writers can add depth and complexity to their characters' interactions, creating a more immersive and engaging reading experience.

3. Build Conflict and Tension

Conflict is at the heart of engaging dialogue, driving the narrative forward and keeping readers invested in the story. ChatGPT can help writers build conflict and tension in their dialogue by generating prompts that explore the characters' conflicting goals, desires, and motivations.

To build conflict and tension with ChatGPT, consider the following strategies:

• Use ChatGPT to generate dialogue prompts that highlight the characters' opposing viewpoints, interests, or agendas.

• Experiment with dialogue prompts that escalate the conflict between characters, leading to confrontations, arguments, or misunderstandings.

• Explore the use of dramatic irony, where the audience knows something that one or more characters do not, to create tension and suspense in the dialogue.

• Use ChatGPT to generate prompts that introduce external conflicts or obstacles that challenge the characters and drive the plot forward.

By building conflict and tension in the dialogue, writers can keep readers on the edge of their seats and compel them to keep turning the pages to see how the conflicts are resolved.

4. Show, Don't Tell

One of the cardinal rules of effective dialogue is to show, rather than tell, the characters' thoughts, feelings, and motivations through their actions and interactions. ChatGPT can assist writers in crafting dialogue that demonstrates the characters' emotions and motivations through vivid and evocative language.

To show, rather than tell, with ChatGPT, consider the following techniques:

• Use ChatGPT to generate dialogue prompts that convey the characters' emotions through their tone of voice, body language, and facial expressions.

• Experiment with descriptive language and sensory details to create vivid imagery and evoke the characters' emotions and surroundings.

• Show the characters' thoughts and feelings through their actions and reactions to the events unfolding around them.

• Use ChatGPT to generate prompts that reveal the characters' motivations and intentions through their dialogue and interactions with other characters.

By showing, rather than telling, in the dialogue, writers can create a more immersive and emotionally resonant reading experience, allowing readers to experience the story through the characters' eyes and emotions.

5. Edit and Revise

Finally, effective dialogue requires careful editing and revision to ensure that every word serves a purpose and contributes to the overall impact of the scene. ChatGPT can assist writers in editing and revising their dialogue by generating prompts that highlight areas for improvement and suggest alternative phrasing or dialogue tags.

To edit and revise dialogue with ChatGPT, consider the following strategies:

• Use ChatGPT to generate prompts that identify weak or redundant dialogue and suggest ways to tighten the dialogue and improve its flow.

• Experiment with different phrasing and word choices to enhance the clarity and impact of the dialogue.

• Seek feedback from beta readers or critique partners on the effectiveness of the dialogue and incorporate their suggestions into your revisions.

• Use ChatGPT to generate prompts that explore alternative dialogue options or scenarios, allowing you to experiment with different approaches and find the most effective way to convey the characters' thoughts and emotions.

By editing and revising the dialogue with ChatGPT, writers can refine their writing and create dialogue that is crisp, compelling, and emotionally resonant, enhancing the overall quality of the narrative.

In conclusion, crafting engaging dialogue requires careful attention to character voice, subtext, conflict, and tension, as well as diligent editing and revision. By leveraging ChatGPT as a tool for dialogue writing, writers can enhance their storytelling skills and create dialogue that captivates readers and brings their characters to life on the page. Whether you're writing a tense confrontation, a heartfelt conversation, or a witty exchange, ChatGPT can assist you in crafting dialogue that resonates with readers and enhances the overall impact of your narrative.

Part 3: Enhancing Dialogue with Emotional Depth and Authenticity

DIALOGUE IS NOT JUST about conveying information or advancing the plot; it's also about evoking emotion and creating connections between characters and readers. In this section, we will explore how writers can use ChatGPT to infuse their dialogue with emotional depth and authenticity, allowing them to create compelling and immersive storytelling experiences that resonate with readers on a visceral level.

1. Explore Characters' Emotional States

Effective dialogue reflects the characters' emotional states and conveys their inner thoughts and feelings to the reader. ChatGPT can help writers explore characters' emotional states by generating prompts that delve into their thoughts, reactions, and emotional responses to the events unfolding in the narrative.

To explore characters' emotional states with ChatGPT, consider the following strategies:

• Use ChatGPT to generate dialogue prompts that reflect the characters' current emotional states, whether it's anger, fear, sadness, joy, or uncertainty.

• Experiment with descriptive language and sensory details to convey the characters' emotions through their physical sensations, such as trembling hands, racing hearts, or churning stomachs.

• Explore the characters' internal monologue and thought processes to reveal their innermost thoughts, fears, and desires.

• Use ChatGPT to generate prompts that explore how the characters' emotional states influence their actions, decisions, and interactions with other characters.

By exploring characters' emotional states with ChatGPT, writers can create dialogue that is rich in depth and authenticity, allowing readers to empathize with the characters and become emotionally invested in their journey.

2. Infuse Dialogue with Subtext and Nuance

Effective dialogue often relies on subtext and nuance to convey meaning and emotion between the lines. ChatGPT can assist writers in infusing their dialogue with subtext and nuance by generating prompts that explore the characters' underlying motives, intentions, and hidden agendas.

To infuse dialogue with subtext and nuance with ChatGPT, consider the following techniques:

• Use ChatGPT to generate prompts that hint at the characters' hidden motives, desires, or secrets, creating intrigue and suspense in the dialogue.

• Experiment with ambiguous or open-ended dialogue prompts that allow for multiple interpretations and layers of meaning.

• Explore the use of metaphor, symbolism, and figurative language to convey complex emotions and themes through the characters' dialogue.

• Use ChatGPT to generate prompts that highlight the characters' conflicting emotions or internal conflicts, adding depth and complexity to the dialogue.

By infusing dialogue with subtext and nuance, writers can create layers of meaning and depth that engage readers and invite them to actively interpret and analyze the text, enhancing their overall reading experience.

1. Develop Authentic Character Relationships

Authentic character relationships are built on a foundation of trust, vulnerability, and mutual understanding. ChatGPT can help writers develop authentic character relationships by generating prompts that explore the dynamics, conflicts, and growth trajectories of their relationships.

To develop authentic character relationships with ChatGPT, consider the following strategies:

• Use ChatGPT to generate dialogue prompts that highlight the characters' shared history, experiences, and memories, deepening their bond and connection.

• Experiment with dialogue prompts that reveal the characters' vulnerabilities, insecurities, and fears, fostering empathy and intimacy between them.

• Explore the characters' communication styles and patterns, as well as their ability to listen, empathize, and support each other through dialogue prompts generated by ChatGPT.

• Use ChatGPT to generate prompts that explore the characters' conflicts and misunderstandings, as well as their efforts to reconcile and resolve their differences.

By developing authentic character relationships with ChatGPT, writers can create dynamic and emotionally resonant dialogue that explores the complexities of human connection and adds depth and richness to the narrative.

4. Convey Theme and Subtext Through Dialogue

Dialogue can serve as a powerful tool for conveying themes and subtext in the narrative, allowing writers to explore complex ideas and concepts through the characters' conversations. ChatGPT can assist writers in conveying theme and subtext through dialogue by generating prompts that explore the underlying themes, motifs, and symbolism present in the narrative.

To convey theme and subtext through dialogue with ChatGPT, consider the following techniques:

- Use ChatGPT to generate dialogue prompts that reflect the central themes and motifs of the narrative, such as love, loss, redemption, or the search for identity.

- Experiment with dialogue prompts that incorporate allegory, metaphor, and symbolism to convey deeper layers of meaning and significance.

- Explore the characters' philosophical beliefs, moral dilemmas, and existential questions through dialogue prompts generated by ChatGPT.

- Use ChatGPT to generate prompts that explore the characters' reactions to the events unfolding in the narrative and their implications for the larger themes and subtext of the story.

By conveying theme and subtext through dialogue, writers can engage readers on a deeper level and invite them to reflect on the broader implications of the narrative, enriching their overall reading experience.

In conclusion, dialogue is a powerful tool for evoking emotion, conveying meaning, and creating connections between characters and readers. By leveraging ChatGPT as a tool for dialogue writing, writers can infuse their dialogue with emotional depth, authenticity, and nuance, enhancing the overall impact and resonance of their narrative. Whether you're exploring characters' emotional states, infusing dialogue with subtext and nuance, developing authentic character relationships, or conveying theme and subtext through dialogue, ChatGPT can assist you in crafting dialogue.

Chapter 4: Setting the Scene: Crafting Vivid and Immersive Settings

Part 1: Establishing Atmosphere and Mood with ChatGPT

CREATING VIVID AND immersive settings is essential for transporting readers to the world of your story, allowing them to experience the sights, sounds, and sensations of the fictional environment. In this section, we will explore how writers can use ChatGPT to establish atmosphere and mood in their settings, drawing readers into the narrative and enhancing their engagement with the story.

1. Descriptive Language and Imagery

Descriptive language and imagery play a crucial role in setting the scene and evoking the sensory experiences of the fictional world. ChatGPT can assist writers in crafting vivid and evocative descriptions by generating prompts that explore the sights, sounds, smells, textures, and colors of the setting.

To use descriptive language and imagery effectively with ChatGPT, consider the following strategies:

• Provide ChatGPT with detailed descriptions of the setting, including its physical features, architectural elements, natural landscape, and atmospheric conditions.

• Use ChatGPT to generate prompts that capture the sensory details of the setting, such as the rustling of leaves in the wind, the scent of pine trees in the forest, or the warmth of sunlight filtering through the clouds.

• Experiment with descriptive language and figurative imagery to create vivid and evocative descriptions that appeal to the reader's senses and imagination.

• Use ChatGPT to generate prompts that explore the emotional impact of the setting on the characters, reflecting their mood, state of mind, and internal conflicts.

By incorporating descriptive language and imagery into the setting with ChatGPT, writers can create a rich and immersive narrative experience that transports readers to the world of their story.

2. Establishing Atmosphere and Mood

Atmosphere and mood are essential elements of setting that influence the tone and emotional resonance of the narrative. ChatGPT can assist writers in establishing atmosphere and mood by generating prompts that explore the sensory details, cultural nuances, and emotional undercurrents of the setting.

To establish atmosphere and mood effectively with ChatGPT, consider the following techniques:

• Use ChatGPT to generate prompts that convey the overall mood and tone of the setting, whether it's a sense of tranquility and serenity in a pastoral landscape or a feeling of foreboding and unease in a dark and ominous forest.

• Experiment with descriptive language and sensory details to create an immersive atmosphere that evokes the emotions and sensations of the setting.

• Explore the cultural and historical context of the setting through dialogue prompts generated by ChatGPT, reflecting its unique traditions, customs, and beliefs.

• Use ChatGPT to generate prompts that explore the characters' reactions to the setting, revealing their emotional responses and adding depth and complexity to their interactions.

By establishing atmosphere and mood with ChatGPT, writers can create a compelling and immersive narrative experience that resonates with readers on an emotional level.

3. Creating a Sense of Place

A sense of place is essential for grounding readers in the setting and creating a tangible and believable world for the story to unfold. ChatGPT can assist writers in creating a sense of place by generating prompts that explore the physical, cultural, and historical aspects of the setting.

To create a sense of place with ChatGPT, consider the following strategies:

• Provide ChatGPT with detailed descriptions of the setting's geography, climate, and topography, as well as its cultural and historical significance.

• Use ChatGPT to generate prompts that highlight the unique features and landmarks of the setting, such as iconic buildings, natural landmarks, or cultural institutions.

• Experiment with descriptive language and sensory details to evoke the specific qualities and characteristics of the setting, whether it's the hustle and bustle of a bustling city street or the serene tranquility of a secluded mountain retreat.

• Use ChatGPT to generate prompts that explore the characters' connections to the setting, reflecting their personal histories, memories, and associations with the place.

By creating a sense of place with ChatGPT, writers can immerse readers in the world of their story and create a vivid and memorable narrative experience that resonates long after they've turned the final page.

1. Incorporating Symbolism and Subtext

Symbolism and subtext can add depth and complexity to the setting, imbuing it with deeper layers of meaning and significance.

ChatGPT can assist writers in incorporating symbolism and subtext into the setting by generating prompts that explore the symbolic elements and thematic motifs present in the narrative.

To incorporate symbolism and subtext with ChatGPT, consider the following techniques:

• Provide ChatGPT with detailed descriptions of the symbolic elements and thematic motifs present in the setting, such as recurring symbols, metaphors, or allegorical references.

• Use ChatGPT to generate prompts that explore the symbolic significance of specific features or landmarks in the setting, reflecting their thematic resonance and symbolic associations.

• Experiment with descriptive language and imagery to convey the deeper layers of meaning and subtext present in the setting, whether it's a dilapidated mansion symbolizing decay and decadence or a lush garden representing renewal and rebirth.

• Use ChatGPT to generate prompts that explore the characters' interactions with the symbolic elements of the setting, revealing their interpretations, insights, and reactions to the symbolic significance of their surroundings.

By incorporating symbolism and subtext into the setting with ChatGPT, writers can enrich the narrative with deeper layers of meaning and resonance, inviting readers to engage with the text on a more profound and thought-provoking level.

In conclusion, establishing atmosphere and mood in the setting is essential for creating a compelling and immersive narrative experience that resonates with readers. By leveraging ChatGPT to explore descriptive language and imagery, establish atmosphere and mood, create a sense of place, and incorporate symbolism and subtext, writers can bring their settings to life on the page and immerse readers in the world of their story. Whether you're crafting a tranquil countryside landscape, a bustling urban metropolis, or a mysterious and otherworldly realm, ChatGPT can assist you in creating vivid and evocative settings that captivate and enchant readers from beginning to end.

Part 2: Developing Dynamic Characters: Using ChatGPT to Create Compelling Personalities

DYNAMIC CHARACTERS are the heart and soul of any story, driving the narrative forward with their actions, motivations, and growth arcs. In this section, we will explore how writers can use ChatGPT to develop dynamic characters that resonate with readers and bring depth and complexity to the narrative.

1. Establishing Character Traits and Attributes

The first step in developing dynamic characters is to establish their core traits and attributes. ChatGPT can assist writers in brainstorming and fleshing out these characteristics by generating prompts that explore the characters' personalities, backgrounds, motivations, and goals.

To establish character traits and attributes with ChatGPT, consider the following strategies:

• Provide ChatGPT with detailed character profiles, including information about each character's physical appearance, personality traits, strengths, weaknesses, and backstory.

• Use ChatGPT to generate prompts that explore the characters' motivations, desires, and goals, as well as the internal and external conflicts that drive them.

• Experiment with descriptive language and imagery to bring the characters to life on the page, conveying their unique quirks, mannerisms, and speech patterns.

• Use ChatGPT to generate prompts that explore the characters' relationships with other characters in the story, revealing their dynamics, conflicts, and alliances.

By establishing character traits and attributes with ChatGPT, writers can create well-rounded and multi-dimensional characters that resonate with readers and drive the narrative forward with their actions and decisions.

2. Crafting Compelling Backstories and Histories

Compelling backstories and histories add depth and complexity to characters, providing insights into their motivations, fears, and vulnerabilities. ChatGPT can assist writers in crafting compelling backstories and histories by generating prompts that explore the characters' past experiences, traumas, and formative moments.

To craft compelling backstories and histories with ChatGPT, consider the following techniques:

• Provide ChatGPT with detailed prompts about the characters' past experiences, including significant events, relationships, and milestones that have shaped their identities and worldviews.

• Use ChatGPT to generate prompts that explore the characters' childhoods, families, and cultural backgrounds, revealing the influences that have shaped their personalities and beliefs.

• Experiment with flashback scenes or memories to delve deeper into the characters' past experiences and emotional journeys.

• Use ChatGPT to generate prompts that explore the characters' reactions to pivotal moments in their lives, such as traumatic events, life-changing decisions, or moments of personal growth and transformation.

By crafting compelling backstories and histories with ChatGPT, writers can create characters with rich and nuanced identities that resonate with readers and add depth and complexity to the narrative.

3. Developing Character Arcs and Growth Trajectories

Character arcs and growth trajectories are essential for depicting the characters' journeys of self-discovery, transformation, and development over the course of the narrative. ChatGPT can assist writers in developing character arcs and growth trajectories by generating prompts that explore the challenges, obstacles, and transformative experiences that shape the characters' evolution.

To develop character arcs and growth trajectories with ChatGPT, consider the following strategies:

• Provide ChatGPT with detailed prompts about the characters' goals, desires, and motivations, as well as the internal and external conflicts that stand in their way.

• Use ChatGPT to generate prompts that explore the characters' reactions to setbacks, failures, and moments of crisis, as well as their efforts to overcome obstacles and achieve their goals.

• Experiment with different narrative structures and plotting techniques to chart the characters' growth trajectories, including the inciting incident, rising action, climax, and resolution.

• Use ChatGPT to generate prompts that explore the characters' relationships with other characters in the story, as well as the impact of these relationships on their growth and development.

By developing character arcs and growth trajectories with ChatGPT, writers can create characters who undergo meaningful and transformative journeys that resonate with readers and add depth and complexity to the narrative.

4. Crafting Memorable Relationships and Interactions

Character relationships and interactions are central to driving the narrative forward and revealing the dynamics, conflicts, and alliances that shape the characters' journeys. ChatGPT can assist writers in crafting memorable relationships and interactions by generating prompts that explore the characters' interpersonal dynamics, conflicts, and emotional connections.

To craft memorable relationships and interactions with ChatGPT, consider the following techniques:

• Provide ChatGPT with detailed prompts about the characters' relationships with other characters in the story, including their dynamics, conflicts, and emotional connections.

• Use ChatGPT to generate prompts that explore the characters' interactions with each other, revealing their communication styles, conflicts, and moments of intimacy or vulnerability.

• Experiment with different types of relationships, including friendships, romances, rivalries, and mentorships, to create dynamic and multi-faceted character dynamics.

• Use ChatGPT to generate prompts that explore the impact of external events and conflicts on the characters' relationships, as well as their efforts to navigate these challenges together.

By crafting memorable relationships and interactions with ChatGPT, writers can create characters whose bonds and connections resonate with readers and add depth and complexity to the narrative.

In conclusion, developing dynamic characters is essential for creating a compelling and immersive narrative experience that resonates with readers. By leveraging ChatGPT to establish character traits and attributes, craft compelling backstories and histories, develop character arcs and growth trajectories, and craft memorable relationships and interactions, writers can create characters that come to life on the page and drive the narrative forward with their actions, motivations, and growth journeys. Whether you're writing a heroic protagonist on a quest for redemption, a complex antagonist grappling with their inner demons, or a diverse ensemble cast navigating the challenges of life and love, ChatGPT can assist you in creating characters that captivate and enchant readers from beginning to end.

Part 3: Enhancing Character Depth and Complexity: Utilizing ChatGPT for Nuanced Portrayals

CHARACTER DEPTH AND complexity are essential for creating compelling and relatable characters that resonate with readers. In this section, we will explore how writers can use ChatGPT to enhance the depth and complexity of their characters, allowing them to create nuanced portrayals that captivate and engage audiences.

1. Exploring Inner Conflicts and Contradictions

Inner conflicts and contradictions add depth and complexity to characters, reflecting the complexities of human nature and the internal struggles we all face. ChatGPT can assist writers in exploring these inner conflicts and contradictions by generating prompts that delve into the characters' desires, fears, insecurities, and moral dilemmas.

To explore inner conflicts and contradictions with ChatGPT, consider the following strategies:

• Provide ChatGPT with detailed prompts about the characters' innermost thoughts, feelings, and motivations, as well as the internal conflicts and contradictions they grapple with.

• Use ChatGPT to generate prompts that explore the characters' moral dilemmas and ethical choices, revealing the complexities of their values, beliefs, and principles.

• Experiment with dialogue prompts that highlight the characters' internal struggles and contradictions, as well as their efforts to reconcile conflicting desires or impulses.

• Use ChatGPT to generate prompts that explore the characters' growth and development over time, as they confront their inner demons and strive to become better versions of themselves.

By exploring inner conflicts and contradictions with ChatGPT, writers can create characters who are complex and multi-dimensional, with layers of depth and complexity that resonate with readers on a profound level.

1. Portraying Authentic Emotions and Vulnerabilities

Authentic emotions and vulnerabilities are essential for creating relatable characters that readers can empathize with and root for. ChatGPT can assist writers in portraying authentic emotions and vulnerabilities by generating prompts that explore the characters' emotional journeys, struggles, and vulnerabilities.

To portray authentic emotions and vulnerabilities with ChatGPT, consider the following techniques:

• Provide ChatGPT with detailed prompts about the characters' emotional experiences, including their hopes, fears, joys, and sorrows, as well as the traumas and wounds that shape their emotional landscape.

• Use ChatGPT to generate prompts that explore the characters' reactions to significant events and milestones in the narrative, as well as their efforts to cope with adversity and overcome obstacles.

• Experiment with descriptive language and imagery to convey the characters' emotional states and inner turmoil, capturing the nuances of their emotional experiences with vivid and evocative language.

• Use ChatGPT to generate prompts that explore the characters' vulnerabilities and insecurities, revealing the fears and doubts that lurk beneath their surface bravado or stoicism.

By portraying authentic emotions and vulnerabilities with ChatGPT, writers can create characters who feel real and relatable, with emotional depth and complexity that resonates with readers on a personal level.

3. Developing Compelling Motivations and Goals

Compelling motivations and goals are essential for driving the characters' actions and decisions, as well as advancing the plot of the narrative. ChatGPT can assist writers in developing compelling motivations and goals by generating prompts that explore the characters' desires, ambitions, and aspirations.

To develop compelling motivations and goals with ChatGPT, consider the following strategies:

• Provide ChatGPT with detailed prompts about the characters' motivations and goals, including their desires, ambitions, and aspirations, as well as the obstacles and challenges they must overcome to achieve them.

• Use ChatGPT to generate prompts that explore the characters' personal stakes and investments in the narrative, revealing the reasons behind their actions and decisions.

• Experiment with dialogue prompts that highlight the characters' conflicts and dilemmas, as well as their efforts to pursue their goals while navigating obstacles and setbacks.

• Use ChatGPT to generate prompts that explore the characters' growth and development over time, as they strive to achieve their goals and fulfill their potential.

By developing compelling motivations and goals with ChatGPT, writers can create characters who are driven and determined, with clear objectives and aspirations that propel the narrative forward and engage readers in their journey.

4. Crafting Authentic Relationships and Dynamics

Authentic relationships and dynamics are essential for creating believable and engaging interactions between characters. ChatGPT can assist writers in crafting authentic relationships and dynamics by generating prompts that explore the characters' connections, conflicts, and emotional bonds.

To craft authentic relationships and dynamics with ChatGPT, consider the following techniques:

• Provide ChatGPT with detailed prompts about the characters' relationships with other characters in the story, including their dynamics, conflicts, and emotional connections.

• Use ChatGPT to generate prompts that explore the characters' interactions and exchanges, revealing the nuances of their communication styles, conflicts, and moments of intimacy or vulnerability.

• Experiment with different types of relationships, including friendships, romances, rivalries, and mentorships, to create dynamic and multi-faceted character dynamics.

• Use ChatGPT to generate prompts that explore the impact of external events and conflicts on the characters' relationships, as well as their efforts to navigate these challenges together.

By crafting authentic relationships and dynamics with ChatGPT, writers can create characters whose bonds and connections resonate with readers, adding depth and complexity to the narrative and enriching the overall reading experience.

In conclusion, enhancing character depth and complexity is essential for creating compelling and relatable characters that resonate with readers. By leveraging ChatGPT to explore inner conflicts and contradictions, portray authentic emotions and vulnerabilities, develop compelling motivations and goals, and craft authentic relationships and dynamics, writers can create characters who feel real and multidimensional, with layers of depth and complexity that engage and captivate audiences from beginning to end. Whether you're writing a protagonist struggling with their inner demons, an antagonist grappling with their moral ambiguity, or a diverse ensemble cast navigating the complexities of relationships and identity, ChatGPT can assist you in creating characters that leave a lasting impression on readers and enrich the narrative with depth and resonance.

51

Chapter 5: Plotting and Pacing: Crafting Compelling Narratives with ChatGPT

Part 1: Building a Solid Foundation: Understanding Plot Structure and Elements

PLOTTING AND PACING are fundamental aspects of storytelling that determine the flow and structure of a narrative. In this section, we will delve into how writers can utilize ChatGPT to craft compelling plots and manage pacing effectively, ensuring that their stories captivate readers from beginning to end.

1. Understanding Plot Structure

Plot structure serves as the backbone of a narrative, providing a framework for organizing events and developing character arcs. ChatGPT can assist writers in understanding and implementing various plot structures by generating prompts that explore the key elements and milestones of each structure.

To understand plot structure with ChatGPT, consider the following strategies:

• Provide ChatGPT with detailed prompts about different plot structures, such as the three-act structure, the hero's journey, or the five-act structure, including the key components and turning points of each structure.

• Use ChatGPT to generate prompts that analyze the structure of well-known stories or novels, identifying the inciting incident, rising action, climax, and resolution, as well as any subplots or secondary arcs.

• Experiment with plotting techniques and plotting tools to outline the plot structure of your own story, using ChatGPT to generate prompts that explore different approaches and possibilities.

• Use ChatGPT to generate prompts that explore the relationship between plot structure and character development, highlighting how the plot impacts the characters' goals, motivations, and growth arcs.

By understanding plot structure with ChatGPT, writers can create narratives that are well-paced, cohesive, and engaging, with a clear sense of direction and purpose.

2. Developing Compelling Story Ideas

Compelling story ideas are the foundation upon which engaging plots are built, providing the inspiration and motivation for writing. ChatGPT can assist writers in developing compelling story ideas by generating prompts that spark creativity and imagination.

To develop compelling story ideas with ChatGPT, consider the following techniques:

• Provide ChatGPT with detailed prompts about different story concepts or premises, including the genre, setting, and central conflict or theme.

• Use ChatGPT to generate prompts that explore various story prompts or plot ideas, encouraging brainstorming and exploration of different narrative possibilities.

• Experiment with different story prompts and plot twists to generate unexpected and intriguing story ideas, using ChatGPT to generate prompts that push the boundaries of conventional storytelling.

• Use ChatGPT to generate prompts that explore the potential implications and consequences of different story ideas, helping to refine and develop them into fully realized plots.

By developing compelling story ideas with ChatGPT, writers can lay the groundwork for engaging plots that captivate readers and keep them invested in the narrative from start to finish.

1. Crafting Engaging Conflict and Tension

Conflict and tension are essential for driving the plot forward and keeping readers engaged and invested in the story. ChatGPT can assist writers in crafting engaging conflict and tension by generating prompts that explore the various types of conflict and techniques for escalating tension.

To craft engaging conflict and tension with ChatGPT, consider the following strategies:

• Provide ChatGPT with detailed prompts about different types of conflict, such as internal conflict, interpersonal conflict, or external conflict, including examples from well-known stories or novels.

• Use ChatGPT to generate prompts that explore techniques for escalating tension and creating suspense, such as foreshadowing, cliffhangers, or dramatic irony.

• Experiment with different plot twists and unexpected developments to introduce new conflicts and obstacles for the characters to overcome, using ChatGPT to generate prompts that explore the potential impact on the plot and character development.

• Use ChatGPT to generate prompts that analyze the relationship between conflict and character growth, highlighting how the challenges and obstacles the characters face contribute to their development and transformation.

By crafting engaging conflict and tension with ChatGPT, writers can create plots that are dynamic, suspenseful, and emotionally resonant, keeping readers on the edge of their seats and eager to see how the story unfolds.

4. Balancing Plot and Subplot

Balancing plot and subplot is essential for creating a well-rounded and cohesive narrative that explores multiple layers of the story. ChatGPT can assist writers in balancing plot and subplot by generating prompts that explore the relationship between the main plot and secondary arcs.

To balance plot and subplot with ChatGPT, consider the following techniques:

• Provide ChatGPT with detailed prompts about different types of subplots, including character-driven subplots, thematic subplots, or subplot arcs that intersect with the main plot.

• Use ChatGPT to generate prompts that analyze the pacing and structure of well-known stories or novels, highlighting how the main plot and subplots are woven together to create a cohesive narrative.

• Experiment with different techniques for integrating subplots into the main plot, such as parallel storytelling, interweaving character arcs, or using subplot arcs to enhance the thematic resonance of the narrative.

• Use ChatGPT to generate prompts that explore the impact of subplots on character development, highlighting how secondary arcs contribute to the overall growth and transformation of the characters.

By balancing plot and subplot with ChatGPT, writers can create narratives that are rich and multi-layered, with depth and complexity that enrich the reading experience and keep readers engaged from beginning to end.

In conclusion, plotting and pacing are essential elements of storytelling that determine the flow and structure of a narrative. By leveraging ChatGPT to understand plot structure, develop compelling story ideas, craft engaging conflict and tension, and balance plot and subplot, writers can create narratives that captivate readers and keep them invested in the story from start to finish. Whether you're writing a thrilling adventure, a poignant romance, or a thought-provoking mystery, ChatGPT can assist you in crafting plots that are dynamic, suspenseful, and emotionally resonant, ensuring that your story leaves a lasting impression on readers long after they've turned the final page.

Part 2: Crafting Dynamic Plot Twists and Resolutions

DYNAMIC PLOT TWISTS and satisfying resolutions are crucial for keeping readers engaged and delivering a fulfilling narrative experience. In this section, we'll explore how writers can use ChatGPT to craft compelling plot twists and resolutions that captivate readers and tie up loose ends effectively.

1. Generating Surprising Plot Twists

Surprising plot twists inject excitement and unpredictability into the narrative, keeping readers on the edge of their seats and eager to uncover what happens next. ChatGPT can assist writers in generating surprising plot twists by generating prompts that explore unexpected developments and unforeseen twists of fate.

To generate surprising plot twists with ChatGPT, consider the following strategies:

• Provide ChatGPT with detailed prompts about the current state of the narrative, including the main characters, their goals, and the conflicts they face.

• Use ChatGPT to brainstorm alternative outcomes and unexpected turns of events that challenge the characters and propel the plot in new and unexpected directions.

• Experiment with different types of plot twists, such as reversals of fortune, shocking revelations, or unexpected alliances, to keep readers guessing and engaged with the story.

• Use ChatGPT to generate prompts that explore the consequences of each plot twist and its impact on the characters, their relationships, and the overall trajectory of the narrative.

By generating surprising plot twists with ChatGPT, writers can create narratives that are full of twists and turns, keeping readers guessing and eager to see how the story unfolds.

2. Resolving Conflicts and Tying Up Loose Ends

Resolving conflicts and tying up loose ends is essential for delivering a satisfying conclusion to the narrative and providing closure for readers. ChatGPT can assist writers in resolving conflicts and tying up loose ends by generating prompts that explore the resolution of key plot points and character arcs.

To resolve conflicts and tie up loose ends with ChatGPT, consider the following techniques:

• Provide ChatGPT with detailed prompts about the unresolved conflicts and loose ends in the narrative, including any lingering questions or unresolved character arcs.

• Use ChatGPT to brainstorm potential resolutions for each conflict and subplot, ensuring that they are consistent with the established plot and character development.

• Experiment with different approaches to resolution, such as redemption arcs, reconciliation, or bittersweet endings, to find the most satisfying conclusion for the narrative.

• Use ChatGPT to generate prompts that explore the aftermath of the resolution, including the characters' reactions, the implications for the world of the story, and any lingering consequences or fallout.

By resolving conflicts and tying up loose ends with ChatGPT, writers can create narratives that feel complete and satisfying, leaving readers with a sense of closure and fulfillment.

3. Crafting Emotional Payoffs and Character Growth

Emotional payoffs and character growth are essential for providing a sense of catharsis and closure for readers, allowing them to connect with the characters on a deeper level and feel invested in their journeys. ChatGPT can assist writers in crafting emotional payoffs and character growth by generating prompts that explore the characters' internal struggles and personal transformations.

To craft emotional payoffs and character growth with ChatGPT, consider the following strategies:

• Provide ChatGPT with detailed prompts about the characters' emotional journeys and growth arcs, including their fears, desires, and inner conflicts.

• Use ChatGPT to brainstorm moments of emotional catharsis and personal revelation for each character, allowing them to confront their demons and overcome their limitations.

• Experiment with different types of character growth, such as self-discovery, forgiveness, or acceptance, to create satisfying arcs that resonate with readers.

• Use ChatGPT to generate prompts that explore the impact of each character's growth on the overall narrative, including how it affects their relationships, their goals, and the resolution of the plot.

By crafting emotional payoffs and character growth with ChatGPT, writers can create narratives that are not only compelling and engaging but also emotionally resonant and deeply satisfying for readers.

1. Creating Thought-Provoking Themes and Messages

Thought-provoking themes and messages add depth and resonance to the narrative, providing readers with insights and reflections that linger long after they've finished reading. ChatGPT can assist writers in creating thought-provoking themes and messages by generating prompts that explore the underlying themes and moral dilemmas of the story.

To create thought-provoking themes and messages with ChatGPT, consider the following techniques:

- Provide ChatGPT with detailed prompts about the central themes and messages of the narrative, including any philosophical or ethical questions the story raises.

- Use ChatGPT to brainstorm scenes and moments that explore these themes in depth, allowing characters to grapple with complex moral dilemmas and existential questions.

- Experiment with different narrative techniques, such as symbolism, allegory, or metaphor, to convey the themes and messages of the story in subtle and evocative ways.

- Use ChatGPT to generate prompts that explore the implications of the story's themes for the characters, the world of the story, and the reader's own life and experiences.

By creating thought-provoking themes and messages with ChatGPT, writers can craft narratives that challenge readers' assumptions and provoke meaningful reflection, elevating the story from mere entertainment to a thought-provoking exploration of the human condition.

In conclusion, crafting dynamic plot twists and resolutions is essential for delivering a compelling and satisfying narrative experience. By leveraging ChatGPT to generate surprising plot twists, resolve conflicts and tie up loose ends, craft emotional payoffs and character growth, and create thought-provoking themes and messages, writers can create narratives that captivate readers and leave a lasting impression long after they've turned the final page. Whether you're writing a thrilling adventure, a poignant romance, or a thought-provoking drama, ChatGPT can assist you in crafting plots that are dynamic, engaging, and emotionally resonant, ensuring that your story resonates with readers and stays with them long after they've finished reading.

Part 3: Refining and Polishing Your Narrative: Utilizing ChatGPT for Revision and Editing

REFINING AND POLISHING your narrative is essential for ensuring that your story is cohesive, engaging, and free of errors. In this section, we'll explore how writers can use ChatGPT to revise and edit their work effectively, improving clarity, coherence, and overall quality.

1. Revising for Clarity and Coherence

Clarity and coherence are essential for ensuring that your narrative is easy to follow and understand. ChatGPT can assist writers in revising for clarity and coherence by generating prompts that highlight areas where the writing may be unclear or confusing.

To revise for clarity and coherence with ChatGPT, consider the following strategies:

• Provide ChatGPT with excerpts from your writing that you suspect may be unclear or confusing, including passages with convoluted syntax, ambiguous language, or inconsistencies in tone or perspective.

• Use ChatGPT to generate prompts that analyze the structure and flow of your writing, highlighting areas where transitions between scenes or paragraphs may be abrupt or disjointed.

• Experiment with different approaches to restructuring sentences or paragraphs to improve clarity and coherence, using ChatGPT to generate prompts that suggest alternative phrasing or organization.

• Use ChatGPT to generate prompts that explore the use of descriptive language and imagery to enhance clarity and evoke a vivid sense of place or character.

By revising for clarity and coherence with ChatGPT, writers can ensure that their narrative is easy to follow and understand, allowing readers to fully engage with the story without getting lost or confused.

2. Editing for Grammar and Style

Editing for grammar and style is essential for ensuring that your writing is polished and professional. ChatGPT can assist writers in editing for grammar and style by generating prompts that identify errors in spelling, punctuation, and grammar, as well as inconsistencies in style and tone.

To edit for grammar and style with ChatGPT, consider the following techniques:

• Provide ChatGPT with excerpts from your writing that you suspect may contain errors in spelling, punctuation, or grammar, including passages with typos, grammatical mistakes, or awkward phrasing.

• Use ChatGPT to generate prompts that analyze the structure and flow of your writing, highlighting areas where sentences may be overly complex or convoluted, or where the tone may be inconsistent or inappropriate for the genre or audience.

• Experiment with different approaches to revising sentences or paragraphs to improve grammar and style, using ChatGPT to generate prompts that suggest alternative word choices or sentence structures.

• Use ChatGPT to generate prompts that explore the use of literary devices and techniques to enhance style and tone, such as metaphor, simile, or parallelism.

By editing for grammar and style with ChatGPT, writers can ensure that their writing is clear, concise, and free of errors, allowing readers to fully immerse themselves in the story without being distracted by technical issues.

3. Strengthening Characterization and Dialogue

Strong characterization and dialogue are essential for bringing your characters to life and making them feel authentic and relatable. ChatGPT can assist writers in strengthening characterization and dialogue by generating prompts that analyze the consistency and authenticity of the characters' voices and interactions.

To strengthen characterization and dialogue with ChatGPT, consider the following strategies:

• Provide ChatGPT with excerpts from your writing that feature character interactions or dialogue, including passages where characters' voices may be inconsistent or where the dialogue may feel forced or unnatural.

• Use ChatGPT to generate prompts that analyze the nuances of the characters' speech patterns, including their vocabulary, syntax, and tone, as well as any regional or cultural influences on their language.

• Experiment with different approaches to developing character voices and dialogue, using ChatGPT to generate prompts that suggest ways to deepen characterizations and make dialogue more authentic and believable.

• Use ChatGPT to generate prompts that explore the emotional subtext of character interactions, highlighting moments of tension, conflict, or intimacy that reveal deeper layers of the characters' personalities and relationships.

By strengthening characterization and dialogue with ChatGPT, writers can create characters who feel real and relatable, with authentic voices and interactions that resonate with readers and draw them deeper into the narrative.

4. Enhancing Descriptive Language and Imagery

Descriptive language and imagery are essential for creating a vivid and immersive narrative experience that transports readers to the world of your story. ChatGPT can assist writers in enhancing descriptive language and imagery by generating prompts that explore ways to evoke sensory experiences and paint vivid mental pictures.

To enhance descriptive language and imagery with ChatGPT, consider the following techniques:

• Provide ChatGPT with excerpts from your writing that feature descriptive passages or imagery, including passages where the language may be bland or generic, or where the imagery may lack detail or specificity.

• Use ChatGPT to generate prompts that analyze the effectiveness of descriptive language and imagery in creating a sense of place or character, highlighting areas where sensory details could be added or expanded upon.

• Experiment with different approaches to crafting descriptive language and imagery, using ChatGPT to generate prompts that suggest specific words or phrases to evoke sensory experiences and paint vivid mental pictures.

• Use ChatGPT to generate prompts that explore the emotional resonance of descriptive language and imagery, highlighting moments where sensory details can enhance the mood or atmosphere of a scene and deepen the reader's emotional connection to the story.

By enhancing descriptive language and imagery with ChatGPT, writers can create a narrative that is rich and immersive, with vivid sensory experiences that bring the world of the story to life and engage readers on a deeper level.

In conclusion, refining and polishing your narrative is essential for ensuring that your story is cohesive, engaging, and free of errors. By utilizing ChatGPT to revise and edit for clarity and coherence, grammar and style, characterization and dialogue, and descriptive language and imagery, writers can create narratives that are polished and professional, with characters who feel real and relatable, and settings that come alive on the page. Whether you're writing a gripping thriller, a heartfelt romance, or an epic fantasy, ChatGPT can assist you in refining and polishing your narrative to perfection, ensuring that your story resonates with readers and leaves a lasting impression long after they've finished reading.

Chapter 6: Crafting Memorable Settings and Atmospheres: Utilizing ChatGPT for World-Building

Part 1: Establishing Immersive Settings: Creating Believable Worlds

CRAFTING MEMORABLE settings and atmospheres is essential for creating a rich and immersive reading experience that transports readers to new worlds and captivates their imagination. In this section, we will explore how writers can use ChatGPT to develop immersive settings and atmospheres that feel authentic and compelling.

1. Establishing the Foundation of Your World

The first step in creating a memorable setting is to establish the foundation of your world. ChatGPT can assist writers in brainstorming and fleshing out the key elements of their fictional worlds by generating prompts that explore the geography, history, culture, and society of the setting.

To establish the foundation of your world with ChatGPT, consider the following strategies:

• Provide ChatGPT with detailed prompts about the geography and climate of your setting, including descriptions of landscapes, terrain features, and weather patterns.

• Use ChatGPT to generate prompts that explore the history and mythology of your world, including significant events, conflicts, and cultural traditions that have shaped its development.

• Experiment with descriptive language and imagery to bring your setting to life on the page, using ChatGPT to generate prompts that evoke the sights, sounds, and smells of your world.

- Use ChatGPT to generate prompts that explore the social structure and hierarchy of your setting, including the roles and responsibilities of different social classes, professions, and factions.

By establishing the foundation of your world with ChatGPT, you can create a setting that feels authentic and immersive, with depth and complexity that resonates with readers and draws them into the story.

1. Developing Unique Cultures and Societies

Unique cultures and societies add depth and richness to your world, providing insights into the beliefs, values, and traditions of its inhabitants. ChatGPT can assist writers in developing unique cultures and societies by generating prompts that explore the customs, rituals, and social norms of different groups within the setting.

To develop unique cultures and societies with ChatGPT, consider the following techniques:

- Provide ChatGPT with detailed prompts about the cultural practices and traditions of different groups within your setting, including ceremonies, festivals, and rites of passage.

- Use ChatGPT to generate prompts that explore the language and dialects spoken by the inhabitants of your world, as well as the symbolism and significance of different words and phrases.

- Experiment with different cultural influences and inspirations to create diverse and multi-faceted societies, using ChatGPT to generate prompts that explore the historical, geographical, and environmental factors that have shaped their development.

- Use ChatGPT to generate prompts that explore the social dynamics and power structures within your world, including the relationships between different social groups, and the sources of conflict and tension that arise from these interactions.

By developing unique cultures and societies with ChatGPT, you can create a setting that feels vibrant and dynamic, with diverse and multi-dimensional characters who reflect the complexity of the world they inhabit.

3. Crafting Evocative Landscapes and Landmarks

Evocative landscapes and landmarks are essential for creating a sense of place and atmosphere in your world, providing readers with vivid mental images that enhance their immersion in the story. ChatGPT can assist writers in crafting evocative landscapes and landmarks by generating prompts that explore the geography, architecture, and natural wonders of the setting.

To craft evocative landscapes and landmarks with ChatGPT, consider the following strategies:

• Provide ChatGPT with detailed prompts about the physical features and landmarks of your setting, including descriptions of cities, towns, villages, and natural landmarks such as mountains, rivers, and forests.

• Use ChatGPT to generate prompts that explore the architectural styles and building materials used in different regions of your world, as well as the cultural and historical significance of different structures and monuments.

• Experiment with descriptive language and imagery to evoke the sensory experiences of your setting, using ChatGPT to generate prompts that capture the sights, sounds, and smells of different landscapes and landmarks.

• Use ChatGPT to generate prompts that explore the role of geography and topography in shaping the development of your world, including how factors such as climate, terrain, and natural resources influence the lives and livelihoods of its inhabitants.

By crafting evocative landscapes and landmarks with ChatGPT, you can create a setting that feels alive and immersive, with rich and detailed descriptions that transport readers to new and exciting places.

4. Infusing Atmosphere and Mood

Atmosphere and mood are essential for creating an emotional connection with your readers and setting the tone for your narrative. ChatGPT can assist writers in infusing atmosphere and mood into their settings by generating prompts that explore the sensory experiences and emotional resonance of different environments.

To infuse atmosphere and mood with ChatGPT, consider the following techniques:

• Provide ChatGPT with detailed prompts about the emotional tone and atmosphere you want to evoke in your setting, including descriptions of the mood, ambiance, and sensory details that contribute to the overall atmosphere.

• Use ChatGPT to generate prompts that explore the use of weather, lighting, and environmental elements to enhance the mood and atmosphere of different scenes and settings.

• Experiment with descriptive language and imagery to evoke specific emotional responses in your readers, using ChatGPT to generate prompts that capture the feelings of awe, wonder, fear, or nostalgia that you want to evoke.

• Use ChatGPT to generate prompts that explore the impact of atmosphere and mood on the characters and their interactions, including how changes in the environment can affect their emotions, behaviors, and decisions.

By infusing atmosphere and mood into your setting with ChatGPT, you can create a narrative that resonates with readers on an emotional level, drawing them into the world of your story and immersing them in its sights, sounds, and sensations.

In conclusion, crafting memorable settings and atmospheres is essential for creating a rich and immersive reading experience that captivates readers and transports them to new worlds. By utilizing ChatGPT to establish the foundation of your world, develop unique cultures and societies, craft evocative landscapes and landmarks, and infuse atmosphere and mood into your setting, you can create a narrative that feels alive and vibrant, with settings that are as dynamic and multi-dimensional as the characters who inhabit them. Whether you're writing a fantastical adventure, a historical epic, or a dystopian thriller, ChatGPT can assist you in crafting settings that captivate readers and leave a lasting impression long after they've finished reading.

Part 2: Creating Dynamic and Interactive Environments

DYNAMIC AND INTERACTIVE environments add depth and realism to your setting, allowing readers to fully immerse themselves in the world of your story. In this section, we'll explore how writers can use ChatGPT to create dynamic and interactive environments that engage readers and enhance their reading experience.

1. Introducing Dynamic Elements

Dynamic elements are essential for creating a sense of life and movement in your setting, making it feel vibrant and dynamic. ChatGPT can assist writers in introducing dynamic elements by generating prompts that explore the various ways in which the environment can change and evolve over time.

To introduce dynamic elements with ChatGPT, consider the following strategies:

• Provide ChatGPT with detailed prompts about the environmental factors that can change and evolve over time, including weather patterns, seasonal changes, and natural disasters.

• Use ChatGPT to generate prompts that explore the impact of human activity on the environment, including deforestation, urbanization, and pollution, as well as the consequences of these changes for the ecosystem and the inhabitants of your world.

• Experiment with descriptive language and imagery to evoke the sensory experiences of dynamic elements, using ChatGPT to generate prompts that capture the sights, sounds, and sensations of environmental changes.

• Use ChatGPT to generate prompts that explore the role of dynamic elements in shaping the plot and character development, including how changes in the environment can create obstacles, challenges, or opportunities for the characters to overcome.

By introducing dynamic elements with ChatGPT, you can create a setting that feels alive and dynamic, with a sense of movement and change that keeps readers engaged and invested in the story.

2. Incorporating Interactive Features

Interactive features are essential for creating a sense of agency and immersion in your setting, allowing readers to actively engage with the environment and influence the course of the narrative. ChatGPT can assist writers in incorporating interactive features by generating prompts that explore the various ways in which readers can interact with the environment.

To incorporate interactive features with ChatGPT, consider the following techniques:

• Provide ChatGPT with detailed prompts about the interactive features you want to include in your setting, including puzzles, challenges, and hidden secrets that readers can discover and explore.

• Use ChatGPT to generate prompts that explore the role of interactive features in shaping the plot and character development, including how readers' choices and actions can impact the outcome of the story.

• Experiment with different types of interactive features, such as branching narratives, choice-based gameplay, or interactive puzzles, to create a sense of agency and immersion for the reader.

• Use ChatGPT to generate prompts that explore the implications of interactive features for the overall narrative structure, including how they can create opportunities for character development, world-building, and plot twists.

By incorporating interactive features with ChatGPT, you can create a setting that feels immersive and engaging, with opportunities for readers to actively participate in the story and shape its outcome.

1. Building Evolving Landscapes

Evolving landscapes are essential for creating a sense of progression and growth in your setting, allowing readers to witness the changes and transformations that occur over time. ChatGPT can assist writers in building evolving landscapes by generating prompts that explore the various stages of development and decay that the environment can undergo.

To build evolving landscapes with ChatGPT, consider the following strategies:

• Provide ChatGPT with detailed prompts about the different stages of development and decay that you want to include in your setting, including the growth of forests, the erosion of mountains, and the rise and fall of civilizations.

• Use ChatGPT to generate prompts that explore the impact of environmental changes on the characters and their interactions, including how shifts in the landscape can create opportunities for exploration, discovery, and conflict.

• Experiment with descriptive language and imagery to evoke the sensory experiences of evolving landscapes, using ChatGPT to generate prompts that capture the sights, sounds, and sensations of growth and decay.

• Use ChatGPT to generate prompts that explore the symbolism and metaphorical significance of evolving landscapes, including how they can reflect the themes and motifs of the story and contribute to its overall meaning.

By building evolving landscapes with ChatGPT, you can create a setting that feels dynamic and alive, with a sense of history and progression that adds depth and richness to the narrative.

4. Integrating Cultural Traditions and Festivals

Cultural traditions and festivals are essential for adding depth and richness to your setting, providing insights into the beliefs, values, and customs of its inhabitants. ChatGPT can assist writers in integrating cultural traditions and festivals by generating prompts that explore the various rituals, ceremonies, and celebrations that take place within the setting.

To integrate cultural traditions and festivals with ChatGPT, consider the following techniques:

• Provide ChatGPT with detailed prompts about the cultural traditions and festivals you want to include in your setting, including descriptions of the rituals, ceremonies, and symbols associated with each celebration.

• Use ChatGPT to generate prompts that explore the significance of cultural traditions and festivals for the characters and their interactions, including how they can serve as points of connection, conflict, or transformation.

• Experiment with descriptive language and imagery to evoke the sensory experiences of cultural traditions and festivals, using ChatGPT to generate prompts that capture the sights, sounds, and sensations of celebration and ceremony.

• Use ChatGPT to generate prompts that explore the role of cultural traditions and festivals in shaping the identity and worldview of the characters, including how they can reflect the values, beliefs, and aspirations of the society as a whole.

By integrating cultural traditions and festivals with ChatGPT, you can create a setting that feels rich and vibrant, with a sense of history and tradition that adds depth and complexity to the narrative.

In conclusion, creating dynamic and interactive environments is essential for enhancing the immersive experience of your setting and engaging readers in the world of your story. By utilizing ChatGPT to introduce dynamic elements, incorporate interactive features, build evolving landscapes, and integrate cultural traditions and festivals, writers can create settings that feel alive and vibrant, with a sense of depth and richness that captivates readers and draws them deeper into the narrative. Whether you're writing a fantastical adventure, a dystopian thriller, or a historical epic, ChatGPT can assist you in creating environments that feel dynamic, interactive, and full of life, ensuring that your story resonates with readers and leaves a lasting impression long after they've finished

Part 3: Evoking Atmosphere and Mood

EVOKING ATMOSPHERE and mood is essential for immersing readers in the world of your story and eliciting emotional responses that deepen their engagement with the narrative. In this section, we'll explore how writers can use ChatGPT to evoke atmosphere and mood effectively, creating a rich and immersive reading experience.

1. Setting the Tone

Setting the tone is the foundation of evoking atmosphere and mood in your narrative. ChatGPT can assist writers in setting the tone by generating prompts that explore the emotional and thematic elements of the story, as well as the overall mood and atmosphere you want to convey.

To set the tone with ChatGPT, consider the following strategies:

• Provide ChatGPT with detailed prompts about the emotional and thematic elements of your story, including the central conflicts, character arcs, and underlying themes.

• Use ChatGPT to generate prompts that explore the tone and mood of different scenes and chapters, including descriptions of the setting, dialogue, and narrative style.

• Experiment with descriptive language and imagery to evoke specific emotional responses in your readers, using ChatGPT to generate prompts that capture the feelings of suspense, excitement, melancholy, or wonder that you want to convey.

• Use ChatGPT to generate prompts that explore the role of tone and mood in shaping the reader's experience of the story, including how changes in atmosphere can affect their emotional engagement and interpretation of events.

By setting the tone with ChatGPT, you can create a narrative that establishes the mood and atmosphere from the very beginning, drawing readers into the world of your story and preparing them for the emotional journey ahead.

2. Creating Vivid Descriptions

Vivid descriptions are essential for bringing your setting to life and immersing readers in its sights, sounds, and sensations. ChatGPT can assist writers in creating vivid descriptions by generating prompts that explore the sensory experiences of different environments and situations.

To create vivid descriptions with ChatGPT, consider the following techniques:

• Provide ChatGPT with detailed prompts about the setting and atmosphere of your story, including descriptions of the sights, sounds, smells, textures, and temperatures that characterize each scene.

• Use ChatGPT to generate prompts that explore the use of descriptive language and imagery to evoke specific sensory experiences, such as the feeling of rain on skin, the scent of pine trees in the forest, or the sound of waves crashing on the shore.

• Experiment with different sensory details and perspectives to create a rich and immersive reading experience, using ChatGPT to generate prompts that suggest alternative ways of describing familiar scenes and situations.

• Use ChatGPT to generate prompts that explore the emotional resonance of descriptive language and imagery, including how sensory details can evoke specific moods and atmospheres that enhance the reader's engagement with the narrative.

By creating vivid descriptions with ChatGPT, you can paint a vivid mental picture for your readers, transporting them to new and exciting places and engaging their senses in the world of your story.

3. Utilizing Symbolism and Metaphor

Symbolism and metaphor are powerful tools for conveying deeper layers of meaning and emotion in your narrative. ChatGPT can assist writers in utilizing symbolism and metaphor by generating prompts that explore the symbolic significance of different objects, settings, and events within the story.

To utilize symbolism and metaphor with ChatGPT, consider the following strategies:

• Provide ChatGPT with detailed prompts about the themes and motifs of your story, including the central symbols and metaphors that you want to incorporate into the narrative.

• Use ChatGPT to generate prompts that explore the symbolic significance of different objects, settings, and events within the story, including how they represent broader themes, ideas, or emotions.

• Experiment with different types of symbolism and metaphor to convey layers of meaning and subtext in your narrative, using ChatGPT to generate prompts that suggest creative ways of incorporating symbolic elements into your writing.

• Use ChatGPT to generate prompts that explore the emotional impact of symbolism and metaphor on the reader, including how they can evoke powerful associations and connections that deepen their engagement with the story.

By utilizing symbolism and metaphor with ChatGPT, you can infuse your narrative with layers of depth and complexity, inviting readers to explore deeper meanings and interpretations that enrich their understanding of the story.

1. Establishing a Sense of Foreboding or Mystery

Establishing a sense of foreboding or mystery is essential for building tension and suspense in your narrative, keeping readers on the edge of their seats and eager to uncover the secrets of the story. ChatGPT can assist writers in establishing a sense of foreboding or mystery by generating prompts that explore the use of atmosphere, pacing, and narrative structure to create suspenseful and enigmatic scenes.

To establish a sense of foreboding or mystery with ChatGPT, consider the following techniques:

• Provide ChatGPT with detailed prompts about the mood and atmosphere you want to create in your narrative, including descriptions of the setting, characters, and events that contribute to the overall sense of tension and suspense.

• Use ChatGPT to generate prompts that explore the use of pacing and narrative structure to build tension and anticipation, including how to introduce clues, red herrings, and plot twists that keep readers guessing and engaged with the story.

• Experiment with different narrative techniques, such as foreshadowing, unreliable narration, or nonlinear storytelling, to create a sense of uncertainty and intrigue, using ChatGPT to generate prompts that explore the potential impact on the reader's experience of the narrative.

• Use ChatGPT to generate prompts that explore the emotional resonance of suspenseful scenes, including how they can evoke feelings of unease, excitement, or curiosity that drive the reader forward and keep them invested in the story.

By establishing a sense of foreboding or mystery with ChatGPT, you can create a narrative that keeps readers guessing and eager to uncover the secrets.

Chapter 7: Developing Compelling Characters: Using ChatGPT for Character Creation

Part 1: Building Multifaceted Characters: Understanding the Basics

DEVELOPING COMPELLING characters is essential for creating a narrative that resonates with readers and keeps them engaged from start to finish. In this section, we'll explore how writers can use ChatGPT to develop multifaceted characters that feel authentic, relatable, and compelling.

1. Understanding Character Archetypes and Tropes

Character archetypes and tropes serve as the foundation for building multifaceted characters, providing writers with familiar frameworks that they can use to develop unique and memorable personalities. ChatGPT can assist writers in understanding character archetypes and tropes by generating prompts that explore the defining traits, motivations, and roles of different character types.

To understand character archetypes and tropes with ChatGPT, consider the following strategies:

• Provide ChatGPT with detailed prompts about common character archetypes and tropes, including descriptions of the hero, the mentor, the villain, the sidekick, and other classic character types.

• Use ChatGPT to generate prompts that analyze the motivations and goals of different character archetypes, as well as the roles they play within the narrative structure.

• Experiment with combining and subverting traditional character archetypes and tropes to create fresh and original personalities, using

ChatGPT to generate prompts that explore alternative interpretations and variations.

• Use ChatGPT to generate prompts that explore the symbolic and thematic significance of different character archetypes, including how they can represent broader themes, ideas, or conflicts within the story.

By understanding character archetypes and tropes with ChatGPT, writers can create characters that feel familiar yet unique, drawing on established conventions while adding their own distinctive twists and nuances.

2. Crafting Compelling Backstories and Motivations

Compelling backstories and motivations are essential for giving characters depth and complexity, allowing readers to understand their actions and empathize with their struggles. ChatGPT can assist writers in crafting compelling backstories and motivations by generating prompts that explore the formative experiences, traumas, and desires that shape each character's identity and worldview.

To craft compelling backstories and motivations with ChatGPT, consider the following techniques:

• Provide ChatGPT with detailed prompts about the backstory and motivations of your characters, including descriptions of their childhoods, family dynamics, personal traumas, and formative experiences.

• Use ChatGPT to generate prompts that explore the psychological and emotional factors that drive each character's behavior, including their fears, desires, insecurities, and moral dilemmas.

• Experiment with different approaches to revealing character backstories and motivations, such as flashback sequences, inner monologues, or dialogue exchanges with other characters, using ChatGPT to generate prompts that explore the most effective methods for conveying this information.

• Use ChatGPT to generate prompts that explore the relationship between each character's backstory and motivations and the overarching themes and conflicts of the story, including how they contribute to the narrative's emotional resonance and thematic depth.

By crafting compelling backstories and motivations with ChatGPT, writers can create characters that feel fully realized and three-dimensional, with rich inner lives and compelling arcs that resonate with readers on a personal level.

3. Developing Complex Relationships and Dynamics

Complex relationships and dynamics are essential for creating dynamic and engaging interactions between characters, driving the plot forward and revealing new layers of depth and complexity in the narrative. ChatGPT can assist writers in developing complex relationships and dynamics by generating prompts that explore the connections, conflicts, and emotional dynamics that define each character's interactions with others.

To develop complex relationships and dynamics with ChatGPT, consider the following strategies:

• Provide ChatGPT with detailed prompts about the relationships between your characters, including descriptions of their histories, shared experiences, conflicts, and emotional bonds.

• Use ChatGPT to generate prompts that analyze the power dynamics and interpersonal conflicts that shape each character's relationships with others, including how they influence their decisions, behaviors, and motivations.

• Experiment with different types of relationships and dynamics, such as friendships, rivalries, romances, or mentor-mentee relationships, using ChatGPT to generate prompts that explore the potential for conflict, growth, and development within each dynamic.

• Use ChatGPT to generate prompts that explore the impact of relationships and dynamics on the overall narrative, including how they drive the plot forward, reveal new aspects of the characters' personalities, and contribute to the thematic resonance of the story.

By developing complex relationships and dynamics with ChatGPT, writers can create interactions between characters that feel authentic and compelling, with layers of tension, intimacy, and emotional depth that keep readers invested in their journeys.

4. Balancing Strengths and Weaknesses

Balancing strengths and weaknesses is essential for creating characters that feel realistic and relatable, with flaws and vulnerabilities that humanize them and make them more compelling. ChatGPT can assist writers in balancing strengths and weaknesses by generating prompts that explore the skills, talents, and limitations of each character, as well as the ways in which they navigate their weaknesses and overcome obstacles.

To balance strengths and weaknesses with ChatGPT, consider the following techniques:

• Provide ChatGPT with detailed prompts about the strengths and weaknesses of your characters, including descriptions of their abilities, talents, flaws, and vulnerabilities.

• Use ChatGPT to generate prompts that explore the ways in which each character's strengths and weaknesses inform their actions and decisions, including how they navigate challenges and overcome obstacles throughout the narrative.

• Experiment with different approaches to character development, such as growth arcs, redemption arcs, or tragic flaws, using ChatGPT to generate prompts that explore the most compelling ways to balance strengths and weaknesses within each character.

• Use ChatGPT to generate prompts that explore the emotional and thematic significance of each character's strengths and weaknesses.

Part 2: Evolving Character Arcs and Growth

CHARACTER ARCS AND growth are essential for creating dynamic and engaging narratives, allowing characters to undergo meaningful transformations over the course of the story. In this section, we'll explore how writers can use ChatGPT to develop evolving character arcs and growth that resonate with readers and drive the plot forward.

1. Establishing Initial Character Traits and Goals

Establishing initial character traits and goals provides a foundation for character development, allowing writers to create protagonists with clear motivations and personalities. ChatGPT can assist writers in establishing initial character traits and goals by generating prompts that explore the desires, fears, and conflicts that drive each character's journey.

To establish initial character traits and goals with ChatGPT, consider the following strategies:

• Provide ChatGPT with detailed prompts about the initial traits and goals of your characters, including descriptions of their personalities, motivations, and ambitions.

• Use ChatGPT to generate prompts that explore the internal and external conflicts that shape each character's journey, including the obstacles they face and the choices they must make to achieve their goals.

• Experiment with different approaches to character development, such as creating characters with conflicting desires or ambiguous moralities, using ChatGPT to generate prompts that explore the potential for growth and change within each character.

• Use ChatGPT to generate prompts that explore the emotional and thematic significance of each character's initial traits and goals, including how they contribute to the overall narrative and thematic resonance of the story.

By establishing initial character traits and goals with ChatGPT, writers can create protagonists with clear motivations and personalities that drive the plot forward and engage readers in their journeys.

1.   Mapping Out Character Development Arcs

Mapping out character development arcs allows writers to plan the trajectory of each character's journey, ensuring that their growth and transformation are both logical and satisfying. ChatGPT can assist writers in mapping out character development arcs by generating prompts that explore the key moments and turning points that shape each character's evolution over the course of the story.

To map out character development arcs with ChatGPT, consider the following techniques:

• Provide ChatGPT with detailed prompts about the key moments and turning points in each character's journey, including descriptions of their growth, setbacks, and revelations.

• Use ChatGPT to generate prompts that explore the internal and external conflicts that drive each character's development, including the challenges they face and the lessons they learn along the way.

• Experiment with different types of character arcs, such as redemption arcs, coming-of-age arcs, or antihero arcs, using ChatGPT to generate prompts that explore the most compelling ways to structure each character's evolution.

• Use ChatGPT to generate prompts that explore the emotional and thematic significance of each character's development arc, including how it contributes to the overall narrative and thematic resonance of the story.

By mapping out character development arcs with ChatGPT, writers can create narratives that feel cohesive and satisfying, with characters who undergo meaningful transformations that resonate with readers.

3. Implementing Growth Through Conflict and Challenges

Implementing growth through conflict and challenges allows characters to confront their weaknesses and overcome obstacles, leading to moments of growth and self-discovery. ChatGPT can assist writers in implementing growth through conflict and challenges by generating prompts that explore the obstacles and setbacks that each character faces, as well as the strategies they use to overcome them.

To implement growth through conflict and challenges with ChatGPT, consider the following strategies:

• Provide ChatGPT with detailed prompts about the conflicts and challenges that each character faces, including descriptions of their internal and external struggles.

• Use ChatGPT to generate prompts that explore the emotional and psychological impact of these conflicts and challenges on each character, including how they force them to confront their fears, insecurities, and limitations.

• Experiment with different types of obstacles and setbacks, such as physical obstacles, moral dilemmas, or interpersonal conflicts, using ChatGPT to generate prompts that explore the most compelling ways to challenge each character's growth.

• Use ChatGPT to generate prompts that explore the strategies and coping mechanisms that each character uses to overcome their obstacles and achieve their goals, including how they learn from their failures and adapt to changing circumstances.

By implementing growth through conflict and challenges with ChatGPT, writers can create narratives that feel dynamic and engaging, with characters who face adversity head-on and emerge stronger and more resilient as a result.

4. Evoking Empathy and Connection Through Vulnerability

Evoking empathy and connection through vulnerability allows readers to empathize with characters' struggles and form emotional connections with them, deepening their engagement with the narrative. ChatGPT can assist writers in evoking empathy and connection through vulnerability by generating prompts that explore the fears, insecurities, and vulnerabilities that each character experiences.

To evoke empathy and connection through vulnerability with ChatGPT, consider the following techniques:

• Provide ChatGPT with detailed prompts about the fears, insecurities, and vulnerabilities that each character experiences, including descriptions of their innermost thoughts and feelings.

• Use ChatGPT to generate prompts that explore the moments of weakness and self-doubt that each character faces, including how they grapple with their flaws and imperfections.

• Experiment with different approaches to vulnerability, such as revealing characters' innermost thoughts and feelings, depicting moments of emotional intimacy or vulnerability, or exploring the impact of trauma and loss on each character's psyche.

• Use ChatGPT to generate prompts that explore the emotional and thematic significance of vulnerability, including how it contributes to the overall narrative and thematic resonance of the story.

By evoking empathy and connection through vulnerability with ChatGPT, writers can create characters that feel authentic and relatable, with struggles and vulnerabilities that resonate with readers on a personal level.

Part 3: Crafting Dynamic Character Relationships

CRAFTING DYNAMIC CHARACTER relationships adds depth and complexity to your narrative, allowing readers to become invested in the interactions between characters and the dynamics that unfold throughout the story. In this section, we'll explore how writers can use ChatGPT to craft dynamic character relationships that feel authentic and compelling.

1. Establishing Chemistry and Conflict

Establishing chemistry and conflict between characters is essential for creating dynamic and engaging relationships that drive the plot forward and keep readers invested in the story. ChatGPT can assist writers in establishing chemistry and conflict between characters by generating prompts that explore the initial impressions, tensions, and interactions that shape their relationships.

To establish chemistry and conflict between characters with ChatGPT, consider the following strategies:

• Provide ChatGPT with detailed prompts about the initial impressions and interactions between characters, including descriptions of their personalities, motivations, and goals.

• Use ChatGPT to generate prompts that explore the tensions and conflicts that arise between characters, including how they clash over differing values, beliefs, or objectives.

• Experiment with different types of chemistry and conflict, such as romantic tension, rivalry, or ideological differences, using ChatGPT to generate prompts that explore the most compelling ways to develop each dynamic.

• Use ChatGPT to generate prompts that explore the emotional and thematic significance of chemistry and conflict, including how they contribute to the overall narrative and thematic resonance of the story.

By establishing chemistry and conflict between characters with ChatGPT, writers can create relationships that feel authentic and dynamic, with layers of tension and complexity that keep readers engaged.

2. Navigating Growth and Change

Navigating growth and change in character relationships allows writers to explore the evolving dynamics between characters as they confront obstacles, overcome challenges, and undergo personal transformations. ChatGPT can assist writers in navigating growth and change in character relationships by generating prompts that explore the challenges, conflicts, and moments of connection that shape each character's journey.

To navigate growth and change in character relationships with ChatGPT, consider the following techniques:

• Provide ChatGPT with detailed prompts about the obstacles and challenges that characters face in their relationships, including descriptions of conflicts, misunderstandings, or betrayals.

• Use ChatGPT to generate prompts that explore the moments of connection and intimacy that characters share, including how they support and challenge each other through adversity.

• Experiment with different approaches to character development, such as growth arcs, reconciliation arcs, or dissolution arcs, using ChatGPT to generate prompts that explore the most compelling ways to evolve each relationship.

• Use ChatGPT to generate prompts that explore the emotional and thematic significance of growth and change in character relationships, including how they contribute to the overall narrative and thematic resonance of the story.

By navigating growth and change in character relationships with ChatGPT, writers can create narratives that feel dynamic and engaging, with relationships that evolve and deepen over time.

1. Developing Compelling Dynamics and Power Struggles

Developing compelling dynamics and power struggles between characters adds depth and tension to your narrative, allowing readers to become invested in the power dynamics and conflicts that unfold throughout the story. ChatGPT can assist writers in developing compelling dynamics and power struggles between characters by generating prompts that explore the hierarchies, rivalries, and conflicts that shape their interactions.

To develop compelling dynamics and power struggles between characters with ChatGPT, consider the following strategies:

• Provide ChatGPT with detailed prompts about the hierarchies and power dynamics that exist between characters, including descriptions of their roles, responsibilities, and areas of influence.

• Use ChatGPT to generate prompts that explore the rivalries and conflicts that arise between characters, including how they compete for resources, recognition, or control.

• Experiment with different types of dynamics and power struggles, such as mentor-protege relationships, love triangles, or political alliances, using ChatGPT to generate prompts that explore the most compelling ways to develop each dynamic.

• Use ChatGPT to generate prompts that explore the emotional and thematic significance of dynamics and power struggles, including how they contribute to the overall narrative and thematic resonance of the story.

By developing compelling dynamics and power struggles between characters with ChatGPT, writers can create relationships that feel nuanced and authentic, with conflicts and tensions that drive the plot forward and keep readers engaged.

4. Resolving Conflict and Building Trust

Resolving conflict and building trust in character relationships allows writers to explore the transformative power of forgiveness, empathy, and reconciliation, as characters overcome past grievances and forge deeper connections with each other. ChatGPT can assist writers in resolving conflict and building trust in character relationships by generating prompts that explore the moments of reconciliation, forgiveness, and understanding that shape their journeys.

To resolve conflict and build trust in character relationships with ChatGPT, consider the following techniques:

• Provide ChatGPT with detailed prompts about the conflicts and misunderstandings that characters must overcome in their relationships, including descriptions of past grievances, betrayals, or misunderstandings.

• Use ChatGPT to generate prompts that explore the moments of reconciliation and forgiveness that characters experience, including how they learn to empathize with each other's perspectives and let go of past resentments.

• Experiment with different approaches to conflict resolution, such as open communication, acts of kindness, or shared experiences, using ChatGPT to generate prompts that explore the most compelling ways to build trust and understanding between characters.

• Use ChatGPT to generate prompts that explore the emotional and thematic significance of conflict resolution and trust-building, including how they contribute to the overall narrative and thematic resonance of the story.

By resolving conflict and building trust in character relationships with ChatGPT, writers can create narratives that feel hopeful and optimistic, with relationships that evolve and deepen over time, ultimately leading to moments of connection and understanding that resonate with readers on a personal level.

In conclusion, crafting dynamic character relationships is essential for creating narratives that feel rich, nuanced, and emotionally resonant. By using ChatGPT to establish chemistry and conflict, navigate growth and change, develop compelling dynamics and power struggles, and resolve conflict and build trust, writers can create relationships that feel authentic and compelling, with layers of complexity and depth that keep readers engaged from start to finish.

Chapter 8: Mastering Dialogue and Character Voice: Using ChatGPT for Authentic Conversations

Part 1: Understanding Dialogue Dynamics and Character Voice

MASTERING DIALOGUE and character voice is essential for creating authentic and engaging conversations that bring your characters to life and drive the plot forward. In this section, we'll explore how writers can use ChatGPT to craft dialogue that feels natural, dynamic, and true to each character's unique voice.

1. Understanding the Purpose of Dialogue

Dialogue serves multiple purposes in storytelling, including revealing character traits, advancing the plot, conveying information, and building tension or conflict. ChatGPT can assist writers in understanding the purpose of dialogue by generating prompts that explore the various functions and dynamics of conversational exchanges within the narrative.

To understand the purpose of dialogue with ChatGPT, consider the following strategies:

• Provide ChatGPT with detailed prompts about the role of dialogue in your story, including descriptions of the characters involved, their motivations, and the context of the conversation.

• Use ChatGPT to generate prompts that analyze the ways in which dialogue reveals character traits, such as personality, background, beliefs, and values.

• Experiment with different types of dialogue, such as exposition, banter, arguments, or confessions, using ChatGPT to generate prompts that explore the most effective ways to achieve your narrative goals.

• Use ChatGPT to generate prompts that explore the relationship between dialogue and other elements of storytelling, such as pacing, tension, and tone, including how they work together to create a cohesive and engaging narrative.

By understanding the purpose of dialogue with ChatGPT, writers can create conversations that feel purposeful, meaningful, and true to the characters and the story's overall direction.

2. Crafting Authentic Character Voices

Crafting authentic character voices is essential for distinguishing between different characters and ensuring that their dialogue feels true to their personalities, backgrounds, and motivations. ChatGPT can assist writers in crafting authentic character voices by generating prompts that explore the unique speech patterns, vocabulary, and mannerisms of each character.

To craft authentic character voices with ChatGPT, consider the following techniques:

• Provide ChatGPT with detailed prompts about the background, personality, and motivations of each character, including descriptions of their speech patterns, vocabulary, and mannerisms.

• Use ChatGPT to generate prompts that analyze the ways in which each character's voice reflects their individuality, including their upbringing, education, social status, and personal experiences.

• Experiment with different approaches to character voice, such as regional dialects, slang, or idiosyncratic speech patterns, using ChatGPT to generate prompts that capture the nuances of each character's voice.

• Use ChatGPT to generate prompts that explore the emotional and thematic significance of character voice, including how it contributes to the overall narrative and thematic resonance of the story.

By crafting authentic character voices with ChatGPT, writers can create conversations that feel immersive, believable, and true to the diverse range of personalities within their narrative.

3. Balancing Dialogue Tags and Action Beats

Balancing dialogue tags and action beats is essential for conveying the rhythm and flow of conversational exchanges, as well as providing clarity and context for readers. ChatGPT can assist writers in balancing dialogue tags and action beats by generating prompts that explore the different ways in which these elements can enhance or detract from the effectiveness of dialogue.

To balance dialogue tags and action beats with ChatGPT, consider the following strategies:

• Provide ChatGPT with detailed prompts about the role of dialogue tags and action beats in your story, including descriptions of their functions, strengths, and potential pitfalls.

• Use ChatGPT to generate prompts that analyze the ways in which dialogue tags and action beats can convey character emotions, reactions, and intentions, including how they contribute to the overall tone and pacing of the conversation.

• Experiment with different types of dialogue tags and action beats, such as descriptive tags, minimalistic tags, or internal monologues, using ChatGPT to generate prompts that explore the most effective ways to use these elements in your writing.

• Use ChatGPT to generate prompts that explore the relationship between dialogue tags, action beats, and other elements of storytelling, such as description, setting, and characterization, including how they work together to create a cohesive and engaging narrative.

By balancing dialogue tags and action beats with ChatGPT, writers can create conversations that feel dynamic, engaging, and easy to follow, with a clear sense of rhythm and flow that keeps readers immersed in the dialogue.

1. Conveying Subtext and Nuance

Conveying subtext and nuance in dialogue adds depth and complexity to conversational exchanges, allowing characters to communicate underlying emotions, motivations, and conflicts without stating them explicitly. ChatGPT can assist writers in conveying subtext and nuance in dialogue by generating prompts that explore the ways in which characters use tone, subtext, and nonverbal cues to convey meaning.

To convey subtext and nuance in dialogue with ChatGPT, consider the following techniques:

• Provide ChatGPT with detailed prompts about the subtextual elements of your dialogue, including descriptions of the characters' underlying emotions, motivations, and conflicts.

• Use ChatGPT to generate prompts that analyze the ways in which characters use tone of voice, body language, and facial expressions to convey subtext and nuance, including how these elements can enrich the reader's understanding of the conversation.

• Experiment with different approaches to conveying subtext and nuance, such as double entendres, irony, or dramatic irony, using ChatGPT to generate prompts that explore the most effective ways to communicate meaning between characters.

• Use ChatGPT to generate prompts that explore the emotional and thematic significance of subtext and nuance in dialogue, including how they contribute to the overall narrative and thematic resonance of the story.

By conveying subtext and nuance in dialogue with ChatGPT, writers can create conversations that feel layered, rich, and full of depth, with a sense of complexity and sophistication that keeps readers engaged and invested in the narrative.

Part 2: Crafting Dynamic Dialogue and Character Voice

CRAFTING DYNAMIC DIALOGUE and character voice is crucial for bringing your characters to life and immersing readers in the world of your story. In this section, we'll delve deeper into how writers can use ChatGPT to craft dialogue that feels authentic, compelling, and true to each character's unique voice.

1. Capturing Character Personality Through Dialogue

Capturing character personality through dialogue involves infusing each character's speech with distinctive traits, quirks, and mannerisms that reflect their individuality. ChatGPT can assist writers in capturing character personality through dialogue by generating prompts that explore the unique speech patterns, vocabulary, and cadences of each character.

To capture character personality through dialogue with ChatGPT, consider the following strategies:

• Provide ChatGPT with detailed prompts about each character's personality traits, background, and motivations, including descriptions of their speech patterns, dialects, and verbal tics.

• Use ChatGPT to generate prompts that analyze the ways in which each character's personality influences their choice of words, sentence structure, and conversational style, including how they express emotions, opinions, and attitudes.

• Experiment with different approaches to character dialogue, such as using slang, dialects, or specialized jargon, using ChatGPT to generate prompts that capture the nuances of each character's voice.

• Use ChatGPT to generate prompts that explore the emotional and thematic significance of character dialogue, including how it contributes to the reader's understanding of the characters' personalities, relationships, and motivations.

By capturing character personality through dialogue with ChatGPT, writers can create conversations that feel authentic, engaging, and true to each character's unique identity.

2. Maintaining Consistency in Character Voice

Maintaining consistency in character voice is essential for ensuring that each character's dialogue remains true to their established personality and traits throughout the narrative. ChatGPT can assist writers in maintaining consistency in character voice by generating prompts that reinforce each character's speech patterns, vocabulary, and mannerisms over the course of the story.

To maintain consistency in character voice with ChatGPT, consider the following techniques:

• Provide ChatGPT with detailed prompts about each character's established speech patterns, vocabulary, and mannerisms, including examples of their dialogue from previous scenes or chapters.

• Use ChatGPT to generate prompts that analyze the ways in which each character's voice evolves or adapts in response to changes in their circumstances, relationships, or motivations, including how they express growth, conflict, or internal conflict through their dialogue.

• Experiment with different methods for tracking and maintaining consistency in character voice, such as creating character profiles or dialogue style guides, using ChatGPT to generate prompts that explore the most effective strategies for your writing process.

• Use ChatGPT to generate prompts that explore the emotional and thematic significance of consistency in character voice, including how it contributes to the reader's immersion in the story and their understanding of the characters' arcs and development.

By maintaining consistency in character voice with ChatGPT, writers can create narratives that feel cohesive, immersive, and true to the diverse range of personalities within their story.

3. Balancing Dialogue and Action

Balancing dialogue and action is essential for creating dynamic and engaging scenes that drive the plot forward and reveal new aspects of the characters' personalities and relationships. ChatGPT can assist writers in balancing dialogue and action by generating prompts that explore the ways in which characters' verbal exchanges are interspersed with physical movements, gestures, or reactions.

To balance dialogue and action with ChatGPT, consider the following strategies:

• Provide ChatGPT with detailed prompts about the pacing and rhythm of your scenes, including descriptions of the balance between dialogue, action, and description.

• Use ChatGPT to generate prompts that analyze the ways in which characters' actions complement or enhance their verbal exchanges, including how they use body language, facial expressions, or gestures to convey emotions, intentions, or subtext.

• Experiment with different techniques for integrating dialogue and action, such as using action beats to break up long stretches of dialogue, or using dialogue tags to convey characters' physical movements or reactions, using ChatGPT to generate prompts that explore the most effective approaches for your narrative.

• Use ChatGPT to generate prompts that explore the emotional and thematic significance of dialogue and action, including how they work together to advance the plot, reveal character dynamics, and create moments of tension or resolution.

By balancing dialogue and action with ChatGPT, writers can create scenes that feel dynamic, immersive, and engaging, with a sense of rhythm and momentum that propels the narrative forward.

4. Conveying Subtext and Emotion Through Dialogue

Conveying subtext and emotion through dialogue allows writers to explore the underlying tensions, conflicts, and motivations that drive characters' interactions and relationships. ChatGPT can assist writers in conveying subtext and emotion through dialogue by generating prompts that explore the ways in which characters use language, tone, and inflection to communicate their feelings and intentions.

To convey subtext and emotion through dialogue with ChatGPT, consider the following techniques:

• Provide ChatGPT with detailed prompts about the subtextual elements of your dialogue, including descriptions of characters' hidden agendas, insecurities, or ulterior motives.

• Use ChatGPT to generate prompts that analyze the ways in which characters' verbal exchanges are layered with underlying meanings, including how they use sarcasm, irony, or ambiguity to convey subtext and emotion.

• Experiment with different approaches to conveying emotion through dialogue, such as using dialogue tags, punctuation, or descriptive language to convey characters' emotional states, using ChatGPT to generate prompts that explore the most effective techniques for your writing style.

• Use ChatGPT to generate prompts that explore the emotional and thematic significance of subtext and emotion in dialogue, including how they contribute to the reader's understanding of the characters' relationships, conflicts, and internal struggles.

By conveying subtext and emotion through dialogue with ChatGPT, writers can create conversations that feel rich, layered, and emotionally resonant, with a sense of depth and complexity that keeps readers invested in the story.

In conclusion, crafting dynamic dialogue and character voice is essential for creating authentic and engaging conversations that bring your characters to life and drive the plot forward. By using ChatGPT to capture character personality, maintain consistency in character voice, balance dialogue and action, and convey subtext and emotion, writers can create scenes that feel immersive, compelling, and true to the diverse range of personalities and relationships within their narrative. Whether you're writing a dramatic confrontation, a tender moment of connection, or a witty exchange of banter, ChatGPT can help you craft dialogue that feels authentic, dynamic, and true to your characters' unique voices.

Part 3: Enhancing Dialogue with Subtext

ENHANCING DIALOGUE with subtext and conflict adds depth, tension, and intrigue to your narrative, enriching character interactions and driving the plot forward. In this section, we'll explore how writers can use ChatGPT to infuse dialogue with subtext and conflict, creating scenes that are emotionally resonant and thematically rich.

1. Infusing Subtext into Dialogue

Infusing subtext into dialogue involves conveying underlying meanings, emotions, and motivations that are not explicitly stated by the characters. ChatGPT can assist writers in infusing subtext into dialogue by generating prompts that explore the ways in which characters use language, tone, and context to communicate hidden agendas, desires, and conflicts.

To infuse subtext into dialogue with ChatGPT, consider the following strategies:

• Provide ChatGPT with detailed prompts about the subtextual elements of your scene, including descriptions of characters' inner thoughts, feelings, and intentions.

• Use ChatGPT to generate prompts that analyze the ways in which characters' verbal exchanges are layered with hidden meanings and implications, including how they use ambiguity, innuendo, or double entendres to convey subtext.

• Experiment with different approaches to conveying subtext through dialogue, such as using metaphor, symbolism, or irony to communicate characters' underlying emotions and motivations, using

ChatGPT to generate prompts that explore the most effective techniques for your narrative.

• Use ChatGPT to generate prompts that explore the emotional and thematic significance of subtext in dialogue, including how it enriches the reader's understanding of the characters' relationships, conflicts, and internal struggles.

By infusing subtext into dialogue with ChatGPT, writers can create scenes that feel layered, nuanced, and emotionally resonant, with a sense of depth and complexity that invites readers to engage with the text on multiple levels.

1. Creating Conflict Through Dialogue

Creating conflict through dialogue involves generating tension, disagreement, or opposition between characters, driving the narrative forward and revealing new layers of conflict and tension. ChatGPT can assist writers in creating conflict through dialogue by generating prompts that explore the ways in which characters' goals, values, and beliefs clash, leading to moments of confrontation, negotiation, or resolution.

To create conflict through dialogue with ChatGPT, consider the following techniques:

• Provide ChatGPT with detailed prompts about the conflicting goals, values, or beliefs of your characters, including descriptions of the stakes, motivations, and consequences of their actions.

• Use ChatGPT to generate prompts that analyze the ways in which characters' verbal exchanges escalate or de-escalate conflicts, including how they use persuasion, manipulation, or coercion to achieve their objectives.

• Experiment with different types of conflict, such as interpersonal conflicts, ideological conflicts, or moral dilemmas, using ChatGPT to generate prompts that explore the most effective ways to generate tension and drama in your scenes.

• Use ChatGPT to generate prompts that explore the emotional and thematic significance of conflict in dialogue, including how it drives character development, advances the plot, and contributes to the overall thematic resonance of the story.

By creating conflict through dialogue with ChatGPT, writers can create scenes that feel dynamic, suspenseful, and emotionally charged, with a sense of urgency and intensity that keeps readers on the edge of their seats.

1. Developing Character Relationships Through Dialogue

Developing character relationships through dialogue involves exploring the dynamics, tensions, and connections that exist between characters, revealing new insights into their personalities, motivations, and conflicts. ChatGPT can assist writers in developing character relationships through dialogue by generating prompts that explore the ways in which characters' verbal exchanges shape their interactions and influence their perceptions of each other.

To develop character relationships through dialogue with ChatGPT, consider the following strategies:

• Provide ChatGPT with detailed prompts about the history, dynamics, and conflicts of your characters' relationships, including descriptions of their past interactions, shared experiences, and unresolved tensions.

• Use ChatGPT to generate prompts that analyze the ways in which characters' verbal exchanges reflect their evolving attitudes, feelings, and perceptions towards each other, including how they navigate moments of intimacy, vulnerability, or conflict.

• Experiment with different types of character relationships, such as friendships, rivalries, or romantic entanglements, using ChatGPT to generate prompts that explore the most compelling dynamics and tensions within each relationship.

• Use ChatGPT to generate prompts that explore the emotional and thematic significance of character relationships in dialogue, including how they contribute to the reader's understanding of the characters' arcs, motivations, and growth.

By developing character relationships through dialogue with ChatGPT, writers can create scenes that feel authentic, immersive, and emotionally resonant, with a sense of intimacy and connection that draws readers deeper into the narrative.

Chapter 9: Crafting Engaging Settings and Descriptions

Part 1: Setting the Scene: Establishing Atmosphere and Immersion

CRAFTING ENGAGING SETTINGS and descriptions is crucial for transporting readers to the world of your story, immersing them in its atmosphere, and bringing its characters and events to life. In this section, we'll explore how writers can use ChatGPT to set the scene effectively, establishing atmosphere and immersion from the very first sentence.

1. Establishing Atmosphere Through Vivid Descriptions

Establishing atmosphere through vivid descriptions involves using sensory details, evocative language, and descriptive imagery to create a sense of time, place, and mood within the narrative. ChatGPT can assist writers in establishing atmosphere through vivid descriptions by generating prompts that explore the sights, sounds, smells, and textures of the setting.

To establish atmosphere through vivid descriptions with ChatGPT, consider the following strategies:

• Provide ChatGPT with detailed prompts about the setting of your scene, including descriptions of its physical features, environmental conditions, and emotional resonance.

• Use ChatGPT to generate prompts that analyze the ways in which sensory details can be used to evoke specific moods, such as tension, serenity, or nostalgia, including how they contribute to the reader's immersion in the story.

- Experiment with different approaches to descriptive language, such as simile, metaphor, or personification, using ChatGPT to generate prompts that capture the essence of the setting in vivid detail.

- Use ChatGPT to generate prompts that explore the emotional and thematic significance of the setting, including how it reflects the characters' internal states, conflicts, and motivations.

By establishing atmosphere through vivid descriptions with ChatGPT, writers can create scenes that feel immersive, atmospheric, and emotionally resonant, with a sense of depth and texture that draws readers deeper into the narrative.

2. Using Setting as a Character

Using setting as a character involves treating the physical environment as an active, dynamic element within the narrative, with its own personality, history, and impact on the story and its characters. ChatGPT can assist writers in using setting as a character by generating prompts that explore the ways in which the environment shapes the actions, emotions, and interactions of the characters.

To use setting as a character with ChatGPT, consider the following techniques:

- Provide ChatGPT with detailed prompts about the role of the setting in your scene, including descriptions of its significance, symbolism, and narrative function.

- Use ChatGPT to generate prompts that analyze the ways in which the environment influences the characters' behavior, attitudes, and decisions, including how it serves as a reflection of their inner states and conflicts.

- Experiment with different ways to personify the setting, such as giving it human-like traits, motivations, or agency, using ChatGPT to generate prompts that explore the most effective approaches for your narrative.

- Use ChatGPT to generate prompts that explore the emotional and thematic significance of the setting as a character, including how it contributes to the reader's understanding of the story's themes, motifs, and underlying messages.

By using setting as a character with ChatGPT, writers can create narratives that feel dynamic, immersive, and thematically rich, with a sense of interconnectedness between the characters, events, and environment that enriches the reader's experience of the story.

3. Creating a Sense of Place and Time

Creating a sense of place and time involves grounding the narrative in a specific location and historical context, allowing readers to visualize and contextualize the events unfolding within the story. ChatGPT can assist writers in creating a sense of place and time by generating prompts that explore the geographical, cultural, and temporal elements of the setting.

To create a sense of place and time with ChatGPT, consider the following strategies:

• Provide ChatGPT with detailed prompts about the geographical features, cultural customs, and historical events that shape the setting of your scene, including descriptions of its location, period, and social context.

• Use ChatGPT to generate prompts that analyze the ways in which the characters' experiences are influenced by the time and place in which they occur, including how they respond to the social norms, political climate, and technological advancements of their environment.

• Experiment with different methods for integrating setting details into the narrative, such as using dialogue, interior monologue, or descriptive passages, using ChatGPT to generate prompts that capture the essence of the time and place in vivid detail.

• Use ChatGPT to generate prompts that explore the emotional and thematic significance of the setting in relation to the characters' journeys, including how it shapes their identities, relationships, and conflicts.

By creating a sense of place and time with ChatGPT, writers can create scenes that feel authentic, immersive, and historically accurate, with a sense of verisimilitude that transports readers to another time and place.

1. Evoking Emotion Through Setting

Evoking emotion through setting involves using descriptive language, symbolism, and imagery to evoke specific emotional responses in the reader, creating a visceral connection to the events and characters of the story. ChatGPT can assist writers in evoking emotion through setting by generating prompts that explore the ways in which the environment can be used to convey mood, tone, and thematic resonance.

To evoke emotion through setting with ChatGPT, consider the following techniques:

• Provide ChatGPT with detailed prompts about the emotional tone and thematic resonance of your scene, including descriptions of the desired mood, atmosphere, and symbolism.

• Use ChatGPT to generate prompts that analyze the ways in which specific setting details can evoke particular emotions, such as fear, awe, or nostalgia, including how they contribute to the reader's emotional engagement with the story.

• Experiment with different approaches to using setting to evoke emotion, such as using contrasting imagery, sensory details, or symbolic motifs, using ChatGPT to generate prompts that explore the most effective techniques for creating emotional resonance in your narrative.

• Use ChatGPT to generate prompts that explore the ways in which the setting can mirror or amplify the characters' internal states and conflicts, including how it reflects their hopes, fears, and desires.

• Experiment with different levels of subtlety and nuance in your descriptions, using ChatGPT to generate prompts that strike the right balance between evocative imagery and narrative restraint.

- Use ChatGPT to generate prompts that explore the emotional and thematic significance of the setting in relation to the overall arc of the story, including how it contributes to the reader's understanding of the characters' journeys and the story's underlying themes.

By evoking emotion through setting with ChatGPT, writers can create scenes that feel visceral, immersive, and emotionally resonant, with a sense of immediacy and intensity that draws readers deeper into the narrative.

In conclusion, crafting engaging settings and descriptions is essential for creating immersive, atmospheric, and emotionally resonant narratives that captivate readers from start to finish. By using ChatGPT to establish atmosphere through vivid descriptions, use setting as a character, create a sense of place and time, and evoke emotion through setting, writers can create scenes that feel alive, vibrant, and richly textured, with a sense of depth and complexity that transports readers to the world of the story. Whether you're writing a sweeping historical epic, a gritty urban thriller, or a fantastical adventure, ChatGPT can help you bring your settings to life in vivid detail, creating a sensory experience that resonates with readers long after they've turned the final page.

Part 2: Developing Rich and Evocative Descriptions

DEVELOPING RICH AND evocative descriptions is essential for painting vivid mental images in the minds of your readers, allowing them to fully immerse themselves in the world of your story. In this section, we'll explore how writers can use ChatGPT to develop descriptions that are both captivating and immersive.

1. Harnessing the Power of Sensory Details

Harnessing the power of sensory details involves appealing to the reader's five senses – sight, sound, smell, taste, and touch – to create a multi-dimensional experience. ChatGPT can assist writers in harnessing the power of sensory details by generating prompts that explore how to effectively incorporate sensory language into descriptions.

To harness the power of sensory details with ChatGPT, consider the following strategies:

• Provide ChatGPT with detailed prompts about the setting or scene you want to describe, including specific sensory experiences you want to evoke.

• Use ChatGPT to generate prompts that explore how to use descriptive language to vividly depict sensory details, such as the colors, textures, sounds, scents, and tastes present in the environment.

• Experiment with different sensory perspectives, such as describing the scene from the viewpoint of a character or an omniscient narrator, using ChatGPT to generate prompts that capture the most immersive and engaging sensory experiences.

• Use ChatGPT to generate prompts that explore the emotional and thematic significance of sensory details, including how they contribute to the mood, tone, and atmosphere of the scene.

By harnessing the power of sensory details with ChatGPT, writers can create descriptions that are rich, immersive, and sensorially engaging, allowing readers to fully experience the world of the story through their imagination.

2. Creating Vivid Imagery and Metaphors

Creating vivid imagery and metaphors involves using language to paint striking mental pictures and draw parallels between disparate elements, adding depth and complexity to descriptions. ChatGPT can assist writers in creating vivid imagery and metaphors by generating prompts that explore how to use descriptive language to evoke powerful visual and conceptual associations.

To create vivid imagery and metaphors with ChatGPT, consider the following techniques:

• Provide ChatGPT with detailed prompts about the scene or object you want to describe, including specific visual or conceptual images you want to evoke.

• Use ChatGPT to generate prompts that explore how to use simile, metaphor, personification, or other literary devices to create vivid and evocative descriptions.

• Experiment with different types of imagery and metaphors, such as nature imagery, sensory imagery, or symbolic imagery, using ChatGPT to generate prompts that capture the most resonant and impactful comparisons.

• Use ChatGPT to generate prompts that explore the emotional and thematic significance of imagery and metaphors, including how they contribute to the reader's understanding of the characters, themes, and underlying messages of the story.

By creating vivid imagery and metaphors with ChatGPT, writers can elevate their descriptions to a new level of richness and complexity, allowing readers to engage with the text on multiple levels and interpret its meaning in their own unique ways.

3. Balancing Description with Narrative Flow

Balancing description with narrative flow involves integrating descriptive passages seamlessly into the overall structure of the narrative, without disrupting the pacing or momentum of the story. ChatGPT can assist writers in balancing description with narrative flow by generating prompts that explore how to effectively weave descriptive language into the fabric of the story.

To balance description with narrative flow with ChatGPT, consider the following strategies:

• Provide ChatGPT with detailed prompts about the pacing and structure of your scene or chapter, including specific moments where you want to incorporate descriptive passages.

• Use ChatGPT to generate prompts that explore how to integrate descriptive language into action sequences, dialogue exchanges, or character interactions, without slowing down the pace of the narrative.

• Experiment with different techniques for transitioning between descriptive passages and other narrative elements, such as using sensory triggers, scene changes, or internal monologue, using ChatGPT to generate prompts that maintain a smooth and seamless narrative flow.

• Use ChatGPT to generate prompts that explore the emotional and thematic significance of description within the context of the larger story, including how it contributes to the reader's immersion in the world of the narrative.

By balancing description with narrative flow with ChatGPT, writers can create a reading experience that feels cohesive, dynamic, and engaging, with descriptions that enhance rather than detract from the overall impact of the story.

4. Invoking Emotion Through Descriptions

Invoking emotion through descriptions involves using language to evoke specific feelings and reactions in the reader, fostering empathy, sympathy, or identification with the characters and events of the story. ChatGPT can assist writers in invoking emotion through descriptions by generating prompts that explore how to use descriptive language to create powerful emotional responses.

To invoke emotion through descriptions with ChatGPT, consider the following techniques:

• Provide ChatGPT with detailed prompts about the emotional tone and thematic resonance of your scene or chapter, including specific emotions you want to evoke in the reader.

• Use ChatGPT to generate prompts that explore how to use descriptive language to convey characters' emotions, such as their physical sensations, internal states, or visceral reactions to their surroundings.

• Experiment with different techniques for evoking emotion, such as using symbolism, foreshadowing, or irony, using ChatGPT to generate prompts that resonate with the reader on a deep and emotional level.

• Use ChatGPT to generate prompts that explore the emotional and thematic significance of descriptions within the larger context of the story, including how they contribute to the reader's understanding of the characters' journeys and the story's underlying themes.

By invoking emotion through descriptions with ChatGPT, writers can create scenes that feel emotionally resonant, immersive, and deeply affecting, allowing readers to connect with the characters and events of the story on a profound level.

In conclusion, developing rich and evocative descriptions is essential for creating immersive, engaging, and emotionally resonant narratives that captivate readers from start to finish. By using ChatGPT to harness the power of sensory details, create vivid imagery and metaphors, balance description with narrative flow, and invoke emotion through descriptions, writers can create a reading experience that feels immersive, dynamic, and deeply satisfying. Whether you're writing a sweeping epic, a gritty thriller, or a tender romance, ChatGPT can help you bring your descriptions to life in vivid detail, creating a sensory experience that resonates with readers long after they've turned the final page.

Part 3: Enhancing Descriptions with Narrative Purpose

ENHANCING DESCRIPTIONS with narrative purpose involves ensuring that every descriptive passage serves a specific function within the larger framework of the story, whether it's advancing the plot, developing character, or reinforcing themes. In this section, we'll explore how writers can use ChatGPT to enhance descriptions with narrative purpose, creating scenes that are not only vivid and immersive but also meaningful and impactful.

1. Advancing the Plot Through Descriptions

Advancing the plot through descriptions involves using descriptive passages to convey crucial information, foreshadow events, or create suspense and tension. ChatGPT can assist writers in advancing the plot through descriptions by generating prompts that explore how to effectively integrate descriptive language into key plot points and narrative developments.

To advance the plot through descriptions with ChatGPT, consider the following strategies:

• Provide ChatGPT with detailed prompts about the plot elements or events you want to describe, including specific details or clues that will drive the story forward.

• Use ChatGPT to generate prompts that explore how to use descriptive language to build suspense, heighten tension, or create dramatic irony, such as describing ominous settings or mysterious objects that foreshadow future developments.

• Experiment with different techniques for integrating descriptive passages into the plot, such as using descriptive imagery to establish the mood or tone of a scene, using ChatGPT to generate prompts that maintain a sense of narrative urgency and momentum.

• Use ChatGPT to generate prompts that explore the emotional and thematic significance of descriptions within the context of the larger plot, including how they contribute to the reader's understanding of the story's themes, motifs, and underlying messages.

By advancing the plot through descriptions with ChatGPT, writers can create scenes that feel dynamic, suspenseful, and tightly woven into the fabric of the narrative, driving readers forward with a sense of anticipation and excitement.

1. Developing Character Through Descriptions

Developing character through descriptions involves using descriptive language to reveal personality traits, motivations, and inner conflicts, allowing readers to connect with the characters on a deeper level. ChatGPT can assist writers in developing character through descriptions by generating prompts that explore how to use descriptive language to bring characters to life in vivid detail.

To develop character through descriptions with ChatGPT, consider the following techniques:

• Provide ChatGPT with detailed prompts about the characters you want to describe, including specific physical features, mannerisms, or quirks that define their personality.

• Use ChatGPT to generate prompts that explore how to use descriptive language to convey characters' emotions, thoughts, and attitudes, such as describing their body language or facial expressions during key moments.

• Experiment with different approaches to character description, such as using indirect characterization techniques to reveal traits through action and dialogue, using ChatGPT to generate prompts that capture the essence of each character in nuanced detail.

• Use ChatGPT to generate prompts that explore the emotional and thematic significance of character descriptions, including how they contribute to the reader's understanding of the characters' arcs, relationships, and growth.

By developing character through descriptions with ChatGPT, writers can create characters that feel fully realized, relatable, and multi-dimensional, with a sense of depth and complexity that enriches the reader's experience of the story.

3. Reinforcing Themes Through Descriptions

Reinforcing themes through descriptions involves using descriptive language to underscore the central ideas, motifs, and messages of the story, creating a cohesive and thematically rich narrative experience. ChatGPT can assist writers in reinforcing themes through descriptions by generating prompts that explore how to use descriptive language to evoke thematic resonance and depth.

To reinforce themes through descriptions with ChatGPT, consider the following strategies:

• Provide ChatGPT with detailed prompts about the themes and motifs you want to explore in your story, including specific symbols, images, or metaphors that embody these concepts.

• Use ChatGPT to generate prompts that explore how to use descriptive language to evoke thematic resonance, such as describing settings or objects that symbolize key themes or ideas.

• Experiment with different approaches to thematic description, such as using recurring imagery or symbolism to create a sense of cohesion and unity, using ChatGPT to generate prompts that reinforce the underlying messages of the story.

• Use ChatGPT to generate prompts that explore the emotional and thematic significance of descriptions within the context of the larger narrative, including how they contribute to the reader's understanding of the story's deeper layers of meaning.

By reinforcing themes through descriptions with ChatGPT, writers can create a narrative that feels thematically rich, intellectually stimulating, and emotionally resonant, with a sense of depth and complexity that invites readers to engage with the text on multiple levels.

4. Creating Atmosphere and Mood Through Descriptions

Creating atmosphere and mood through descriptions involves using descriptive language to evoke specific emotions, moods, and sensations in the reader, immersing them in the world of the story and enhancing their emotional engagement with the narrative. ChatGPT can assist writers in creating atmosphere and mood through descriptions by generating prompts that explore how to use descriptive language to set the tone and ambiance of a scene.

To create atmosphere and mood through descriptions with ChatGPT, consider the following techniques:

• Provide ChatGPT with detailed prompts about the desired atmosphere and mood of your scene, including specific sensory details or emotional states you want to evoke.

• Use ChatGPT to generate prompts that explore how to use descriptive language to create a sense of place, time, and ambiance, such as describing weather patterns, lighting conditions, or environmental elements that contribute to the mood of the scene.

• Experiment with different techniques for evoking atmosphere and mood, such as using descriptive imagery to establish a sense of foreboding or mystery, using ChatGPT to generate prompts that capture the emotional essence of the scene.

• Use ChatGPT to generate prompts that explore the emotional and thematic significance of atmosphere and mood within the context of the larger narrative, including how they contribute to the reader's immersion in the world of the story.

By creating atmosphere and mood through descriptions with ChatGPT, writers can create scenes that feel immersive, atmospheric, and emotionally resonant, with a sense of depth and complexity that draws readers deeper into the narrative.

In conclusion, enhancing descriptions with narrative purpose is essential for creating immersive, engaging, and thematically rich narratives that captivate readers from start to finish. By using ChatGPT to advance the plot, develop character, reinforce themes, and create atmosphere and mood through descriptions, writers can create scenes that are not only vivid and immersive but also meaningful and impactful, with a sense of depth and complexity that resonates with readers long after they've turned the final page. Whether you're writing a sweeping epic, a gritty thriller, or a poignant romance, ChatGPT can help you bring your descriptions to life in vivid detail, creating a sensory experience that transports readers to the heart of your story.

Chapter 10: Polishing Your Prose: Editing and Revision Techniques

Part 1: Understanding the Importance of Editing and Revision

UNDERSTANDING THE IMPORTANCE of editing and revision is crucial for refining your prose, polishing your manuscript, and elevating the overall quality of your writing. In this section, we'll explore why editing and revision are essential steps in the writing process and how they can help you craft a stronger, more compelling narrative.

1. Honing Your Craft: Improving Clarity and Cohesion

Honing your craft through editing and revision involves refining your writing to enhance clarity, cohesion, and readability. ChatGPT can assist writers in honing their craft by generating prompts that focus on improving sentence structure, eliminating redundancy, and clarifying confusing passages.

To hone your craft through editing and revision with ChatGPT, consider the following strategies:

• Provide ChatGPT with detailed prompts about the specific areas of your manuscript that you want to improve, including passages that feel awkward, unclear, or repetitive.

• Use ChatGPT to generate prompts that explore how to rephrase sentences for clarity and conciseness, such as simplifying complex language or breaking up long, convoluted sentences into shorter, more digestible chunks.

• Experiment with different techniques for improving cohesion and flow, such as using transitional phrases, parallel structure, or varied sentence lengths, using ChatGPT to generate prompts that enhance the overall readability of your prose.

• Use ChatGPT to generate prompts that analyze the effectiveness of your writing style and voice, including how to maintain consistency and authenticity throughout your manuscript.

By honing your craft through editing and revision with ChatGPT, you can refine your prose to a higher level of clarity, coherence, and professionalism, ensuring that your manuscript is engaging and accessible to readers.

2. Strengthening Your Story:

Enhancing Plot and Characterization

Strengthening your story through editing and revision involves revisiting the fundamental elements of your narrative, such as plot, characterization, and pacing, to ensure that they are cohesive, compelling, and emotionally resonant. ChatGPT can assist writers in strengthening their story by generating prompts that focus on refining plot twists, deepening character development, and tightening pacing.

To strengthen your story through editing and revision with ChatGPT, consider the following techniques:

• Provide ChatGPT with detailed prompts about the key plot points, character arcs, and thematic elements of your manuscript that you want to enhance or clarify.

• Use ChatGPT to generate prompts that explore how to streamline your plot, eliminate subplots or scenes that detract from the main storyline, and tighten pacing to maintain narrative momentum.

• Experiment with different approaches to character development, such as giving characters distinct voices, motivations, and conflicts, using ChatGPT to generate prompts that deepen their complexity and emotional depth.

• Use ChatGPT to generate prompts that analyze the thematic resonance of your story, including how to reinforce central themes, motifs, and messages throughout your manuscript.

By strengthening your story through editing and revision with ChatGPT, you can create a narrative that is tightly plotted, emotionally resonant, and thematically cohesive, drawing readers in and keeping them engaged from beginning to end.

1. Polishing Your Prose: Enhancing Style and Voice

Polishing your prose through editing and revision involves fine-tuning your writing style and voice to create a distinctive and compelling authorial presence. ChatGPT can assist writers in polishing their prose by generating prompts that focus on refining language, enhancing imagery, and strengthening narrative voice.

To polish your prose through editing and revision with ChatGPT, consider the following strategies:

• Provide ChatGPT with detailed prompts about the tone, mood, and atmosphere you want to evoke in your manuscript, including specific stylistic elements or literary devices you want to incorporate.

• Use ChatGPT to generate prompts that explore how to enhance descriptive imagery, metaphorical language, and sensory details to create a vivid and immersive reading experience.

• Experiment with different techniques for crafting a unique authorial voice, such as varying sentence structure, rhythm, and pacing, using ChatGPT to generate prompts that capture the essence of your personal style.

• Use ChatGPT to generate prompts that analyze the effectiveness of your prose in conveying emotion, tone, and thematic resonance, including how to strike the right balance between exposition and dialogue, narration and action.

By polishing your prose through editing and revision with ChatGPT, you can refine your writing style and voice to a higher level of sophistication and artistry, creating a narrative that is not only engaging and immersive but also distinctively your own.

4. Revisiting Your Vision: Aligning with Your Goals and Intentions

Revisiting your vision through editing and revision involves reassessing your goals, intentions, and creative vision for the manuscript, ensuring that your final draft aligns with your original vision while also incorporating feedback and insights gained through the editing process. ChatGPT can assist writers in revisiting their vision by generating prompts that encourage reflection, self-assessment, and strategic decision-making.

To revisit your vision through editing and revision with ChatGPT, consider the following techniques:

• Provide ChatGPT with detailed prompts about your creative goals, thematic intentions, and narrative vision for the manuscript, including specific areas where you feel your current draft may deviate from your original vision.

• Use ChatGPT to generate prompts that explore how to incorporate feedback from beta readers, critique partners, or editors while also staying true to your artistic vision and voice.

• Experiment with different approaches to revising your manuscript, such as restructuring scenes, reimagining characters, or rethinking plot twists, using ChatGPT to generate prompts that help you make strategic decisions that align with your creative goals.

• Use ChatGPT to generate prompts that analyze the thematic coherence and emotional resonance of your manuscript, including how to ensure that every element of your story contributes to the overarching narrative arc and thematic resonance.

By revisiting your vision through editing and revision with ChatGPT, you can ensure that your final manuscript is a faithful expression of your creative vision and intent, polished to a high standard of quality and ready to share with readers and publishers alike.

In conclusion, understanding the importance of editing and revision is essential for refining your prose, strengthening your story, and aligning with your creative vision. By honing your craft, strengthening your story, polishing your prose, and revisiting your vision through editing and revision with ChatGPT, you can elevate the overall quality of your writing and create a manuscript that is engaging, immersive, and thematically resonant. Whether you're a seasoned author or a novice writer, ChatGPT can help you navigate the complexities of the editing process and transform your rough draft into a polished masterpiece that captivates readers and leaves a lasting impression.

Part 2: Techniques for Effective Editing and Revision

EFFECTIVE EDITING AND revision require a structured approach that focuses on identifying and addressing key areas of improvement within your manuscript. In this section, we'll explore specific techniques and strategies that writers can use to streamline their editing process and maximize the impact of their revisions.

1. Establishing Clear Editing Goals

Establishing clear editing goals is essential for guiding your revision process and ensuring that you focus on the most critical areas of improvement within your manuscript. ChatGPT can assist writers in establishing clear editing goals by generating prompts that encourage reflection, self-assessment, and strategic decision-making.

To establish clear editing goals with ChatGPT, consider the following strategies:

• Provide ChatGPT with detailed prompts about your editing priorities, including specific aspects of your manuscript that you want to improve, such as plot, characterization, pacing, or prose style.

• Use ChatGPT to generate prompts that encourage you to set specific, measurable, achievable, relevant, and time-bound (SMART) editing goals, such as revising a certain number of chapters per day or focusing on a particular aspect of craft for each editing session.

• Experiment with different approaches to goal-setting, such as breaking down your editing goals into smaller, more manageable tasks, using ChatGPT to generate prompts that help you stay organized and focused throughout the revision process.

• Use ChatGPT to generate prompts that analyze the effectiveness of your editing goals in addressing the weaknesses and shortcomings of your manuscript, including how to adapt and adjust your goals as needed based on feedback and insights gained during the editing process.

By establishing clear editing goals with ChatGPT, you can create a roadmap for your revision process that guides your efforts and helps you stay on track toward achieving your desired outcomes.

2. Conducting Comprehensive Manuscript Assessments

Conducting comprehensive manuscript assessments involves critically evaluating every aspect of your manuscript, from plot and pacing to character development and prose style, to identify strengths, weaknesses, and areas for improvement. ChatGPT can assist writers in conducting comprehensive manuscript assessments by generating prompts that encourage careful analysis, reflection, and self-assessment.

To conduct a comprehensive manuscript assessment with ChatGPT, consider the following techniques:

• Provide ChatGPT with detailed prompts about the specific aspects of your manuscript that you want to evaluate, including strengths you want to build upon and weaknesses you want to address.

• Use ChatGPT to generate prompts that encourage you to read your manuscript with a critical eye, identifying inconsistencies, plot holes, and narrative inconsistencies that may detract from the overall impact of your story.

• Experiment with different approaches to manuscript assessment, such as creating checklists, spreadsheets, or mind maps to track your observations and insights, using ChatGPT to generate prompts that help you organize and prioritize your revision efforts.

• Use ChatGPT to generate prompts that analyze the effectiveness of your manuscript in achieving your creative goals and intentions, including how to leverage strengths and mitigate weaknesses to create a more compelling and cohesive narrative.

By conducting a comprehensive manuscript assessment with ChatGPT, you can gain valuable insights into the strengths and weaknesses of your manuscript, allowing you to make informed decisions about where to focus your revision efforts for maximum impact.

3. Implementing Structural and Content Edits

Implementing structural and content edits involves making substantive changes to your manuscript, such as revising plot points, developing characters, or restructuring scenes, to improve overall coherence and effectiveness. ChatGPT can assist writers in implementing structural and content edits by generating prompts that encourage strategic decision-making, creative problem-solving, and narrative development.

To implement structural and content edits with ChatGPT, consider the following strategies:

• Provide ChatGPT with detailed prompts about the specific structural and content issues you want to address within your manuscript, including plot holes, pacing problems, and character inconsistencies.

• Use ChatGPT to generate prompts that explore different approaches to revising your manuscript, such as brainstorming new plot twists, reimagining character arcs, or restructuring scenes to improve narrative flow and coherence.

• Experiment with different techniques for implementing structural and content edits, such as outlining, storyboarding, or using index cards to visualize your manuscript's structure and identify areas for improvement, using ChatGPT to generate prompts that guide your creative process.

• Use ChatGPT to generate prompts that analyze the effectiveness of your structural and content edits in addressing the weaknesses and shortcomings of your manuscript, including how to integrate feedback and insights from beta readers, critique partners, or editors into your revision process.

By implementing structural and content edits with ChatGPT, you can strengthen the foundation of your manuscript and ensure that it is structurally sound, thematically cohesive, and emotionally resonant.

1. Polishing Language and Style

Polishing language and style involves refining your prose to enhance clarity, coherence, and literary merit, ensuring that every word serves a purpose and contributes to the overall impact of your narrative. ChatGPT can assist writers in polishing language and style by generating prompts that focus on improving sentence structure, enhancing descriptive imagery, and strengthening narrative voice.

To polish language and style with ChatGPT, consider the following techniques:

• Provide ChatGPT with detailed prompts about the specific aspects of your prose that you want to polish, including sentence-level issues such as awkward phrasing, repetitive language, or passive voice constructions.

• Use ChatGPT to generate prompts that explore different techniques for improving language and style, such as varying sentence structure, using active voice, or incorporating literary devices such as metaphor, simile, and symbolism to enhance descriptive imagery and narrative depth.

• Experiment with different approaches to polishing language and style, such as reading your manuscript aloud, soliciting feedback from critique partners or beta readers, or using editing software to identify common writing pitfalls and stylistic weaknesses, using ChatGPT to generate prompts that guide your revision process.

• Use ChatGPT to generate prompts that analyze the effectiveness of your language and style edits in enhancing the overall impact of your narrative, including how to strike the right balance between clarity and complexity, simplicity and sophistication.

By polishing language and style with ChatGPT, you can elevate the quality of your prose to a higher level of sophistication and artistry, creating a narrative that is not only engaging and immersive but also aesthetically pleasing and emotionally resonant.

In conclusion, employing techniques for effective editing and revision is essential for refining your manuscript, strengthening your story, and maximizing the impact of your writing. By establishing clear editing goals, conducting comprehensive manuscript assessments, implementing structural and content edits, and polishing language and style with ChatGPT, you can create a narrative that is engaging, immersive, and thematically resonant, with a sense of depth and complexity that captivates readers and leaves a lasting impression. Whether you're a seasoned author or a novice writer, ChatGPT can help you navigate the complexities of the editing process and transform your rough draft into a polished masterpiece that shines with literary brilliance.

Part 3: Refining Your Editing Process for Efficiency and Effectiveness

REFINING YOUR EDITING process involves optimizing your workflow and adopting strategies that help you work more efficiently and effectively, ultimately leading to a stronger and more polished manuscript. In this section, we'll explore techniques and practices that writers can use to streamline their editing process and achieve their revision goals with greater ease.

1. Establishing a Structured Editing Workflow

Establishing a structured editing workflow is essential for staying organized and focused throughout the revision process. ChatGPT can assist writers in establishing a structured editing workflow by generating prompts that encourage strategic planning, time management, and task prioritization.

To establish a structured editing workflow with ChatGPT, consider the following strategies:

• Provide ChatGPT with detailed prompts about your editing process, including specific tasks you need to complete and deadlines you need to meet.

• Use ChatGPT to generate prompts that help you break down your revision goals into smaller, more manageable tasks, such as revising individual chapters, developing character arcs, or polishing prose style.

• Experiment with different approaches to task prioritization, such as using a checklist, calendar, or project management software to track your progress and stay on schedule, using ChatGPT to generate prompts that help you allocate your time and resources effectively.

• Use ChatGPT to generate prompts that analyze the effectiveness of your editing workflow in achieving your revision goals, including how to adapt and adjust your process as needed based on feedback and insights gained during the revision process.

By establishing a structured editing workflow with ChatGPT, you can create a roadmap for your revision process that guides your efforts and helps you stay on track toward achieving your desired outcomes.

2. Utilizing Feedback and Critique

Utilizing feedback and critique is essential for gaining fresh perspectives on your manuscript and identifying areas for improvement that may not be immediately apparent to you as the author. ChatGPT can assist writers in utilizing feedback and critique by generating prompts that encourage collaboration, dialogue, and constructive criticism.

To utilize feedback and critique with ChatGPT, consider the following techniques:

• Provide ChatGPT with detailed prompts about the specific aspects of your manuscript that you want feedback on, including plot points, character development, prose style, and thematic resonance.

• Use ChatGPT to generate prompts that encourage you to seek feedback from a variety of sources, such as beta readers, critique partners, writing groups, or professional editors, using ChatGPT to generate prompts that guide your communication and collaboration with others.

• Experiment with different approaches to receiving and processing feedback, such as soliciting specific questions or prompts to focus feedback on particular areas of concern, using ChatGPT to generate prompts that help you interpret and integrate feedback into your revision process.

• Use ChatGPT to generate prompts that analyze the effectiveness of the feedback you receive in identifying strengths and weaknesses within your manuscript, including how to prioritize and implement suggested revisions in a way that aligns with your creative vision and intentions.

By utilizing feedback and critique with ChatGPT, you can gain valuable insights into the strengths and weaknesses of your manuscript, allowing you to make informed decisions about where to focus your revision efforts for maximum impact.

3. Embracing Iterative Revision

Embracing iterative revision involves recognizing that the editing process is an ongoing and iterative journey, with each round of revisions bringing you closer to your desired outcome. ChatGPT can assist writers in embracing iterative revision by generating prompts that encourage flexibility, adaptability, and openness to change.

To embrace iterative revision with ChatGPT, consider the following strategies:

• Provide ChatGPT with detailed prompts about your willingness to revise and refine your manuscript, including how you approach feedback, incorporate new ideas, and adapt your vision as needed.

• Use ChatGPT to generate prompts that encourage you to view revision as a natural and essential part of the writing process, rather than a sign of failure or inadequacy, using ChatGPT to generate prompts that foster a growth mindset and a willingness to learn and grow as a writer.

• Experiment with different approaches to iterative revision, such as revisiting earlier drafts of your manuscript to mine for overlooked gems or exploring alternative narrative paths and possibilities, using ChatGPT to generate prompts that spark creativity and experimentation.

• Use ChatGPT to generate prompts that analyze the effectiveness of your iterative revision process in refining your manuscript and achieving your creative goals, including how to recognize when a piece is ready for publication and when it still needs further refinement and polish.

By embracing iterative revision with ChatGPT, you can approach the editing process with a sense of curiosity, exploration, and discovery, allowing your manuscript to evolve and improve with each round of revisions.

4. Celebrating Progress and Milestones

Celebrating progress and milestones is essential for maintaining motivation and momentum throughout the editing process. ChatGPT can assist writers in celebrating progress and milestones by generating prompts that acknowledge achievements, milestones, and breakthroughs.

To celebrate progress and milestones with ChatGPT, consider the following techniques:

• Provide ChatGPT with detailed prompts about the specific achievements and milestones you want to celebrate, such as completing a round of revisions, receiving positive feedback, or reaching a word count milestone.

• Use ChatGPT to generate prompts that encourage you to acknowledge and celebrate your progress, no matter how small or seemingly insignificant, using ChatGPT to generate prompts that foster a sense of pride, accomplishment, and satisfaction.

• Experiment with different approaches to celebrating progress and milestones, such as rewarding yourself with small treats or indulgences, sharing your achievements with friends or writing communities, or simply taking a moment to reflect on how far you've come, using ChatGPT to generate prompts that help you cultivate a positive and affirming mindset.

• Use ChatGPT to generate prompts that analyze the effectiveness of your celebration rituals in boosting morale and maintaining motivation throughout the editing process, including how to incorporate celebration into your workflow in a way that feels meaningful and authentic.

By celebrating progress and milestones with ChatGPT, you can stay motivated and inspired throughout the editing process, fueling your creativity and driving you toward your ultimate goal of producing a polished and publishable manuscript.

In conclusion, refining your editing process for efficiency and effectiveness is essential for achieving your revision goals and creating a manuscript that is polished, compelling, and ready for publication. By establishing a structured editing workflow, utilizing feedback and critique, embracing iterative revision, and celebrating progress and milestones with ChatGPT, you can streamline your editing process and maximize the impact of your revisions, ultimately leading to a stronger and more polished manuscript. Whether you're a seasoned author or a novice writer, ChatGPT can help you navigate the complexities of the editing process and transform your rough draft into a polished masterpiece that shines with literary brilliance.

Finale:

FIRST OFF, I WOULD like to thank you for taking the time to read this book and support me!

Writing books, wether with Ai or the old fashioned way, takes patience, care and love for what you do.

It is not easy to come up with a good story or a solid piece of instructional wording, even with Ai. Ai is not 100% reliable and is not quite a big force to be reckoned with in the book writing business. What it Ai does do, is give non authors a voice, allowing them to tell their stories and share their advice!

I hope this has given you all the information you need to get you novel to where you want it to be! Best of luck!